American
English in Mind

Herbert Puchta & Jeff Stranks

Combo 2A Student's Book

CAMBRIDGE
UNIVERSITY PRESS

CAMBRIDGE UNIVERSITY PRESS
Cambridge, New York, Melbourne, Madrid, Cape Town,
Singapore, São Paulo, Delhi, Mexico City

Cambridge University Press
32 Avenue of the Americas, New York, NY 10013-2473, USA

www.cambridge.org
Information on this title: www.cambridge.org/9780521733458

First published 2011
5th printing 2013

Printed in Hong Kong, China, by Sheck Wah Tong Printing Press Limited

A catalogue record for this publication is available from the British Library.

ISBN 978-0-521-73344-1 Student's Book 2
ISBN 978-0-521-73345-8 Combo 2A
ISBN 978-0-521-73346-5 Combo 2B
ISBN 978-0-521-73350-2 Workbook 2
ISBN 978-0-521-73351-9 Teacher's Edition 2
ISBN 978-0-521-73352-6 Class Audio 2
ISBN 978-0-521-73328-1 Classware 2
ISBN 978-0-521-73353-3 Testmaker 2
ISBN 978-0-521-73365-6 DVD 2

Art direction, book design and layout: Pentacor plc
Photo research: Pronk and Associates

Contents

Unit	Grammar	Vocabulary	Pronunciation
1 My interesting life	Simple present; present continuous; *like, love, enjoy + -ing*; *have to / don't have to*; simple past; count and noncount nouns; *much/many*; *some/any*; comparative and superlative adjectives	Hobbies and interests; jobs; food; two-word verbs	Word stress
2 Looking into the future	*will/won't*; *too + adjective*; adverbs; *be going to*; first conditional; *should/shouldn't*; present perfect with *ever/never*	Expressions to talk about the future; future time expressions; the weather; adjectives for feelings and opinions; personality adjectives	/ɪ/ and /aɪ/
CHECK YOUR PROGRESS			
3 Great idea!	Past continuous; past continuous vs. simple past, *when* and *while*	*get*	*was* and *were*
4 He ran faster.	Comparative and superlative adjectives; intensifiers with comparatives; *(not) as ... as*; adverbs / comparative adverbs	Antonyms; sports	*than* and *as*
CHECK YOUR PROGRESS			
5 Our world	*will/won't*; *might (not) / may (not)* for prediction; *if/unless + first conditional*	The environment	/oʊ/ *won't*
6 Holiday or vacation?	Tag questions; present perfect; *just/already/yet*	British vs. North American English	Intonation in tag questions
CHECK YOUR PROGRESS			
7 Growing up	Present passive; *let / be allowed to*	Describing a person's age	/aʊ/ *allowed*
8 Have fun!	Present perfect; *for* vs. *since*	Verb and noun pairs	*have, has* and *for*
CHECK YOUR PROGRESS			

Pages 114–122   Pronunciation • Speaking exercises • Projects • Irregular verbs

SCOPE AND SEQUENCE

Speaking & Functions	Listening	Reading	Writing
Ordering in a restaurant Talking about unusual hobbies	A story about an "unforgettable experience"	Blog entry Email text: At a restaurant Culture in mind: Interesting hobbies	Essay about a hobby
Giving advice Last but not least: talking about school summer vacations	Conversation: Trying something new	Text messages about future plans Photostory: Where's my cell phone?	Essay about your summer vacation
Describing past activities Talking about listening to music	Science fiction story	Article: What did they invent? Article: Be an inventor! Culture in mind: The history of listening to music	Story about invention
Making comparisons Last but not least: talking about sports	Talk: Olympic medalists	Article: Australia: Almost the champions Photostory: A marathon	Report about a sports event
Discussing environmental problems Predicting future events Talking about using water responsibly	Song: *Big Yellow Taxi* Culture in mind: Water as a natural resource	Article: Bicycle revolution?	Website article about your town
Checking information Asking people questions about habits, routines, likes, and dislikes Last but not least: exchanging information about the U.S. and Canada	Answering a quiz about the U.S. and Canada Conversation about things recently done	Quiz: The U.S. and Canada Comment posts: Is free wireless Internet a good idea for Vancouver? Photostory: New girl	Email about a vacation
Describing a coming of age ceremony Retelling a story Talking about: permission; minimum age limits	Story from Papua New Guinea Dialogue about minimum ages Quiz about minimum ages	Article: Where boys become crocodile men Quiz: How old do you have to be? Culture in mind: Coming of age in Japan	Magazine article about a special day
Expressing different points of view on playing Talking about: ongoing situations; Are you fun to be with? Last but not least: talking about having fun and laughing	Song: *Don't Worry, Be Happy*	Article: The power of play Questionnaire: Are you fun to be with? Photostory: Very funny!	Email about how you have fun

1 My interesting life

* Grammar: simple present; present continuous; *like, love, enjoy* + *-ing*; *have to / don't have to*; simple past; count and noncount nouns; *much/many*; *some/any*; comparative and superlative adjectives
* Vocabulary: hobbies and interests; jobs; food; two-word verbs

1 Read and listen

a Do you have a blog? If you do, what kinds of things do you write about? If you don't, would you like to have one? Why or why not? Tell a partner.

b ▶ **CD1 T02** Read and listen to Brian's blog entry. What is he worried about?

NEW BLOG ENTRY

March 29th

I'm writing this in my room. It's almost midnight, and I have to get up early tomorrow, but I can't sleep. I'm worried about my future! Every day, my parents ask me, "What do you want to be when you grow up?" The problem is: I don't know! My mom always says, "Be a doctor!" But to be a doctor, you have to study for a long, long time, and that's not my idea of fun. Also, I'm really bad at biology at school. My dad says, "Be a pilot!" He knows I'm scared of flying! Besides, a pilot has to be really good at math. I like math, but I'm not very good at it.

Well, I have some ideas, of course. I really want to be a rock star. You don't have to be very smart – at least not smart in things like math and science. So it's the perfect job for me. I don't play any instruments, but I can probably learn. My singing isn't too bad, either.

Now I'm getting tired, and my fingers hurt, too. So I'm going to bed. I can think about my future in bed. I get my best ideas when I'm lying down. Or maybe one more computer game? Decisions, decisions, decisions!

c Read the blog entry again. Answer the questions.

1 What time is it?
2 Why can't Brian sleep?
3 Why doesn't he want to be a doctor?
4 Why doesn't he want to be a pilot?
5 Why is a rock star the perfect job for him?
6 Why is he going to bed?

d Complete the sentences with the correct forms of *have to* or *don't have to*.

1 Doctors _____ study for a long time.
2 Pilots _____ study biology.
3 Most rock stars _____ play the guitar or be good singers.
4 Brian's parents say that he _____ think about his future.
5 Brian's mom says, "Be a doctor!" but he _____ be a doctor.
6 Brian _____ go to bed because he's too tired to write.

e Work with a partner. Ask and answer the questions.

1 What do you think? Can Brian be a rock star? Why or why not?
2 What do you think is a good job for Brian? Why?

Grammar review

✳ Simple present

a Write the verbs in the correct form of the simple present.

1 We _____eat_____ eggs for breakfast every day. (eat)

2 Our teacher always _____ us homework on Fridays. (give)

3 My father _____ baseball. (not like)

4 _____ all your friends _____ to the same school? (go)

5 Where _____ your best friend _____ ? (live)

✳ Present continuous

b Complete the email with the correct form of the present continuous.

```
  _____  _□□✕

  Hi, Sally!

  It's me, Jessica. I ¹ __'m writing__
  (write) to you from Brazil! We
  ² _____ (stay) in a nice hotel
  near the beach. I ³ _____ (have)
  a really good time. It's a beautiful day
  today. The sun ⁴ _____ (shine)
  and my brother and sister
  ⁵ _____ (play) on the beach. Me?
  I ⁶ _____ (not do) any work!

  Love,
  Jessica
```

✳ Simple present vs. present continuous

c Read the telephone conversation. <u>Underline</u> the correct choices.

Andy: Hi Sophie. It's me, Andy. What ¹ *do you do / are you doing* ?

Sophie: Not much. Why?

Andy: Do you want to go to the movies with me? I ² *go / am going* every Friday.

Sophie: Well, I don't know. I can only go after eight o'clock. We always ³ *have / are having* dinner at 7:30. My mom ⁴ *cooks / is cooking* dinner now.

Andy: OK. Let's meet at the theater at 8:15.

Sophie: That sounds good! OK, well, I'll see you at 8:15. Thanks for calling.

✳ *like, love, enjoy + -ing* (hobbies and interests)

		¹D							
			²G	O	I	N	G		
³S									
		⁴P							
	⁵R								
⁶P									
⁷L									
		⁸R							

d Complete the clues in the text and fill in the puzzle. What's the mystery word?

My friend Jane and I have lots of hobbies and interests. We really like ² ___going___ to the movies on weekends. Both of us like ⁷ _____ to music, too, and we love ¹ _____ at parties if the music's really good! Jane's better at music than I am. She enjoys ⁴ _____ the guitar.

We like different sports and subjects. Jane enjoys ⁵ _____ in the park, but I like ³ _____ in the pool. I like ⁶ _____ pictures in art class, but Jane's favorite subject is English because she loves ⁸ _____ books.

❸ Vocabulary review

✳ Jobs

Put the letters in the correct order to find the jobs. Write the jobs under the correct pictures.

hacitterc   netidts   orocdt
thlifg tentatdan   relawy   lipot

1 _____

2 _____

3 _____

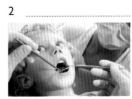
4 _____

5 _____

6 _____

4 Read and listen

a Read the email. Why was their visit to the restaurant an "unforgettable experience"?

Hi, Olivia!

You can't imagine what happened last night. Dad took us out to a famous expensive restaurant, but there weren't many people there last night. Their website says that the restaurant is "An unforgettable experience." Well, it certainly was unforgettable!

We ordered the "exotic surprise" and thought it was going to be wonderful, but it was the most awful meal I've ever had! The first course was chicken and French fries! The chicken was bad, but the fries were worse. Yuck!

Then they gave us something called "ham with strawberries." When the waiter brought it, there was one little ham sandwich and just one strawberry on each plate. And you won't believe what happened next. The waiter tried to put the plates on the table, but he dropped one. And then the worst thing happened! He picked the sandwich up from the floor, put it back on the plate and gave it to Mom. Mom asked him to throw the sandwich away. "Aren't you hungry?" the waiter asked. My dad got really angry, but the waiter only laughed! I tried the ice cream for dessert. Yuck! (I didn't eat much.)

Next time we'll take you to the same restaurant! Just kidding! ;-)

Your friend,

Tom

b Read the text again and listen. Write *T* (true) or *F* (false).

1 Tom and his family went to a fast-food restaurant. ☐

2 They didn't like their first course at all. ☐

3 The ham came with a lot of strawberries. ☐

4 Tom's mother didn't want her sandwich. ☐

5 The waiter was very sorry and apologized. ☐

6 Tom liked the ice cream. ☐

5 Grammar review

✳ Simple past: regular and irregular verbs

a Complete the conversation with the simple past of the verbs. Then practice with a partner.

A: _____*Did*_____ you ____*watch*____ the movie on TV last night? (watch)

B: Well, I [1] _____ (want) to watch it, but then Natalie [2] _____ (come over), and we [3] _____ (go) to see the baseball game at the stadium. [4] _____ (be) the movie good?

A: Not really. The actors [5] _____ (be) so bad that I [6] _____ (fall) asleep after 20 minutes. And when I [7] _____ (wake) up, I only [8] _____ (see) the last two minutes of the movie.

B: I'm glad I [9] _____ (not stay) home.

A: [10] _____ you _____ (enjoy) the game?

B: Well, you won't believe this, 20 minutes into the game, it [11] _____ (start) to rain. My team [12] _____ (lose) zero to three, and then we [13] _____ (miss) the last bus home.

A: So how [14] _____ you _____ (get) home? [15] _____ you _____ (call) your dad?

B: No, I didn't. We [16] _____ (take) a taxi, and we [17] _____ (pay) $10 each. So now I have no money until the end of the month!

✳ Count and noncount nouns (food vocabulary)

b Work with a partner. Add as many items to the lists as you can.

vegetables:	onions, carrots, …
fruit:	apples, …
appetizers:	vegetable soup, …
main courses:	grilled fish, …
desserts:	ice cream, …
drinks:	milk, …

c Which of the words in your lists are count nouns (e.g., apples, carrots), and which are noncount (e.g., milk, fruit)? Make lists with your partner.

count	noncount
onions	

6 Speak

Work in groups. Imagine you are in a restaurant ordering food and drinks. One of you is the waiter. Act out a conversation.

7 Grammar review

✳ *much/many*

a Underline the correct word in each sentence.

1 How *much / many* money do you want to spend?
2 We don't have *much / many* time.
3 I don't want *much / many* carrots.
4 She couldn't get *much / many* information.
5 He doesn't have *much / many* friends.

✳ *some/any*

b Complete the sentences with *some* or *any*.

1 I wanted to make myself ___*some*___ vegetable soup, but there weren't ___*any*___ vegetables left.
2 If you're hungry, have _____ sandwiches.
3 We bought _____ rice, but we didn't buy _____ tomatoes.
4 A: Let's have _____ dessert.
   B: Great. Do we have _____ ice cream?
5 A: Can I have _____ sugar in my coffee?
   B: I'm really sorry, but we don't have _____ sugar at home.

✳ Comparative and superlative adjectives

c Complete the sentences with the comparative or superlative forms of the adjectives.

1 I heard about your exam grades. You must be the ___*happiest*___ person in the world right now. (happy)
2 Mexico City is one of the _____ cities in the world, but Tokyo is even _____ . (big)
3 I think George Clooney is the _____ actor. I think he's much _____ than Brad Pitt. (good)
4 This is one of the _____ movies I have ever seen. I think it's _____ than the movie we saw two weeks ago. (interesting)
5 I thought losing all my money was the _____ experience of my life, but this situation is _____ than that. (bad)

8 Vocabulary review

✳ Two-word verbs

Complete the sentences with the correct forms of the two-word verbs from the box.

give up	check out	~~take up~~
look up	figure out	

1 He's already playing in a band, and he only ___*took up*___ playing the guitar a year ago!
2 He has _____ candy, and now he's much thinner.
3 I can't remember what this word means. I'll have to _____ it _____ in a dictionary.
4 I just can't _____ the answer to this math problem.
5 I've heard there's a new pizza place in town. Why don't we _____ it _____ ?

9 Pronunciation

▶ **CD1 T04 and T05** Pronunciation section starts on page 114.

Culture in mind

10 Read and listen

a Work with a partner. Ask and answer the questions.

1 What are your favorite hobbies or free-time activities?
2 Why is it important for people to have hobbies?

b Read the article and choose the best title for it.

1 The same dull hobbies
2 Yarn bombing
3 New and exciting hobbies

Are you tired of people asking the question, "What's your favorite hobby?" You always hear the same old answers: reading, listening to music, painting and so on. There's nothing wrong with these activities, but maybe it's time for some new ideas.

For example, how about yarn bombing? What's that? Well, maybe you have heard of knitting to make sweaters, scarves, gloves and other things. With yarn bombing, people knit different kinds of things, like sweaters for trees or a hat for the statue in the park. It's the latest form of urban artwork. In some cities, people are even paying knitters to decorate public places with their art. Some call it "Knitting Graffiti," but unlike other forms of graffiti, it is easy to remove, and it doesn't damage anything.

Do you like those TV shows where the police use science to solve crimes? If you do, you can take up forensic science as a hobby. (That's the science used to investigate crimes.) You can get an at-home fingerprint kit and find out who is taking cookies from the cookie jar or perhaps who is reading your secret diary.

Finally, here's a hobby for those who want to have fun and make a little money. It's called "upcycling." You've heard of *recycling* where you put things like glass, paper and plastic in special bins so the materials can be used again. Upcyclers take old things and make them into new things. Sometimes they can even sell the things they make. For example, you can take an old book bag, clean it up and decorate it. It will look like a cool new bag. Or you can make pencil holders out of recycled cans. There's even a magazine called *Upcycle* that is full of ideas. All you need for this is old stuff and a good imagination.

So look around for a new and interesting hobby. Then when someone asks you the question "What's your hobby?" you can give them an answer they've never heard before.

c ▶ CD1 T06 Read the article again and listen. Write the letter of the correct hobby after each phrase.

a yarn bombing   b forensic science   c upcycling

1 Make old things new: _c_
2 Make a scarf for a statue: ....
3 Find out who used your cell phone: ....
4 Decorate something old: ....
5 Solve crimes at home: ....

Vocabulary

Complete the sentences. Use the words in the box.

> bin   decorate   fingerprints   graffiti   ~~knitting~~   solve

1   Did you know that men, not women, invented the art of ___knitting___ ? They used it to make nets to catch fish.

2   Some kids wrote _____ on the school walls. The principal says they have to clean it off.

3   In real life, the police don't _____ every crime like they do on the TV shows.

4   I know you drank from this glass. It has your _____ on it!

5   Please throw those glass bottles and soda cans in the recycling _____ .

6   I'm going to _____ this old book bag with pictures of stars and planets and call it a "Space Bag."

 ## Speak

Work in a group. Ask and answer the questions.

1   Some people think that yarn bombing is a fun kind of art. Other people don't like it. They think that people shouldn't put sweaters on trees or statues. What do you think? Why?

2   What new hobbies can you think of? Give three ideas.

13 Write

a   Read Brenda's essay about a new hobby.

b   Read the essay again. Answer the questions.

1   What is Brenda's hobby?

2   Why does she like this hobby?

3   What kinds of things does Brenda do for this hobby?

4   What does Brenda want to do in the future?

c   How does Brenda collect insects? Number the steps in the correct order.

_____   She looks at the insect with a magnifying glass.

___1___   She finds an insect near her house or in the park.

_____   She puts the insect in a bottle.

_____   She takes the insect back and lets it go.

_____   She draws a picture of the insect.

_____   She reads about the insect in a book.

d   Write an essay about one of your hobbies or about a hobby you want to have. Use Brenda's essay and the questions in Exercise 13b to help you.

My new hobby

I started a new hobby this year. My hobby is collecting insects. I've always liked insects. They are interesting, and they can be very beautiful.

I find insects in many different places, such as the yard around my house or the park near my school. When I see a new insect, I put it in a glass bottle. I look at it very carefully. If it's small, I use a magnifying glass. Then I try to find out what kind of an insect it is. I have a lot of books about insects to help me. After that, I draw a picture of it in my notebook. I also write its name, the date and where I found it. Finally, I take it back to the same place and let it go. I don't keep it.

Some day I want to be an entomologist. That's a person who studies insects. Then my hobby will be my job!

2 Looking into the future

* Grammar: *will/won't*; *too* + adjective; adverbs; *be going to*; first conditional; *should/shouldn't*; present perfect with *ever/never*
* Vocabulary: expressions to talk about the future; future time expressions; the weather; adjectives for feelings and opinions; personality adjectives

1 Read and listen

a What kinds of things do your parents say no to? Why? Tell a partner.

b Read the messages. What is Jane and Tony's problem?

Hi Jane,

Ken and I are going to play beach volleyball tomorrow afternoon. Are you going to come? They say it'll be hot tomorrow. But not too hot for volleyball!

Hope to see you there,

Tony

Hi T!

Not sure. I'll check with my mom right now. She'll probably say yes. (If I come, I want to be on your team, no matter what . . . !)

Jane

Too bad! Guess what my mom said: "All you do is play beach volleyball! You're going to get bad grades." Anyway, have fun. I don't think you'll win without me!

Jane :-(

Relax. My mother just talked to me. I can't go either. Parents!

Anyway, I hope to see you on Sat! Movies??

Tony ;-)

c ▶ CD1 T07 Read again and listen. Write the names next to the sentences.

1 Who would like to go to the beach?

....

2 Who can't go to the beach? ....

3 Who says the weather's going to be nice?

....

4 Who thinks his/her mother will say OK?

....

5 When does Tony hope to go to the movies?

....

d Make true sentences about the notes. Use *will* or *won't* and the verb in parentheses.

1 Tony says that it .... (be) hot tomorrow.

2 Then he says it .... (be) too hot to play volleyball.

3 At first, Jane thinks that her mother .... (say) yes.

4 I doubt that Tony and Jane .... (play) volleyball tomorrow.

5 Tony and Jane .... probably .... (go) to the movies on Saturday.

Grammar review

✱ too + adjective

a Complete each sentence. Use *too* and an adjective from the box.

big   cold   expensive   fast   ~~young~~

1 I can't go in there. You have to be 17, so I'm
   ......*too young*...... .

2 Can I try a smaller size, please? This one's
   ....

3 Let's stay here and sit by the fire. It's
   .... to go outside.

4 Slow down! You're walking .... !
   I can't keep up with you!

5 One hundred dollars for this T-shirt? I'm sorry,
   that's ....

✱ Adverbs

b Write sentences using the correct form of a verb from A and the adverb form of an adjective from B.

A: play   run   ~~walk~~   cook
B: fast   good   loud   ~~quiet~~

1 We came home very late, so we ......*walked*......
   into the house very ......*quietly*...... .

2 The band last night .... so
   .... that we all got headaches.

3 The dog .... so ....
   that Gerry couldn't catch it.

4 I like eating Sara's food. She ....
   ....

Vocabulary review

✱ Expressions to talk about the future

a Use the words in the box to complete the sentences.

doubt   hope   maybe   probably

1 I don't know what I'm going to do tomorrow,
   but .... I'll just stay at home.

2 I .... to see you tomorrow or
   the day after tomorrow.

3 Helen doesn't like sports very much, so I
   .... she'll come to the game
   with us.

4 I .... won't go out tonight. I'm
   too tired from last night!

✱ Future time expressions

b Which expression can replace the underlined words? (Circle) the correct words.

1 It's 7:00. I'm going out at 10:00.
   (*in three hours*) / *for three hours*

2 It's Saturday today. School starts again
   on Monday.
   the day after tomorrow / the next day

3 It's November. I'm going on vacation
   in December.
   next month / the next month

4 It's May 10th. My birthday is on May 24th.
   next week / in two weeks

5 It's 2011 now. I'm going to graduate from high
   school in 2015.
   the year after next / in four years

✱ The weather

c Do the crossword puzzle.

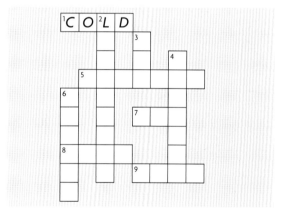

1 It was very ......*cold*...... last night – only 3°C.

2 Did you see that? There was a bright flash of
   ....

3 It's not as hot now. The .... has
   gone behind the clouds.

4 Let's watch the .... forecast on
   TV and see what tomorrow will be like.

5 There was a big storm last night. Did you hear
   the .... ?

6 It wasn't heavy rain. It was just a
   ....

7 It's too .... to sit on the beach.
   Let's go for a swim!

8 It was difficult to walk because of the
   .... in our faces.

9 This is how I like it, not hot, not cold, just
   nice and .... !

4 Read and listen

▶ CD1 T08 Read and listen to the conversation. What is William going to do next week? Why?

William: Guess what? Next week, I'm going to start diving lessons! You know, scuba diving.

Sam: Really? That's cool! But I'm surprised. Have you ever done anything like this before?

William: No, never. And that's the problem. My life's really boring. I'm really boring. Well, that's what Emily Jones said yesterday.

Sam: Well, that was pretty rude. Emily is cute, but she can be mean sometimes. Wait a minute – are you doing this because of her?

William: No! Well, uh, I'm not sure. Kind of. Maybe. Well, yes.

Sam: You're crazy! You shouldn't do things just to impress other people. Especially Emily Jones!

William: I know, but I like her. I've never taken a risk in my life. And if I don't take any risks, I'll never get what I want.

Sam: OK. So tell me, if you go diving, will you enjoy it?

William: Probably not. To be honest, I'm really scared! And ... well, the truth is, I can't swim!

5 Speak

Should William take diving lessons? Role-play a conversation with a partner. One of you is Sam, the other William. Sam gives William advice.

6 Pronunciation

▶ CD1 T09 Pronunciation section starts on page 114.

7 Grammar review

❋ First conditional

a Read the conversation and complete the sentences. Put the verbs in parentheses into the correct form.

A: Let's go downtown.

B: No, I have to do this homework. If I ¹ _go_ (go) downtown, I ¹ _won't finish_ (not finish) it today.

A: So what?

B: Well, if I ² _____ (not finish) it today, I ³ _____ (not give) it to the teacher tomorrow.

A: I see, and if you ⁴ _____ (not give) it to her, she ⁵ _____ (be) angry with you.

B: That's right.

A: Well, I ⁶ _____ (be) angry with you if you ⁷ _____ (not go) downtown with me.

B: Oh, no! Look, if I ⁸ _____ (go) with you, ⁹ _____ you _____ (help) me later with the homework?

A: OK! It's a deal!

✱ should/shouldn't

b Complete each dialogue. Use *should* or *shouldn't* and a phrase from the box.

> go this evening ~~ask your parents~~ be more polite
>
> go to school eat a bigger breakfast be more relaxed

1 A: I'm going to take scuba-diving lessons.

B: Oh? Well, I think you *should ask your parents* .

2 A: Ellie and Josh are hungry – again!

B: Well, maybe they .... in the morning.

3 A: Are you worried about the test tomorrow?

B: Yes, a little. I think I .... about it.

4 A: Let's go for a walk in the park.

B: No, it's almost dark. We

....

5 A: I have a really bad cold.

B: Well, you .... today.

6 A: I don't know why he's so angry with me.

B: It's because you were rude to him. You

.... , you know.

✱ Present perfect with *ever/never*

c Complete the questions and answers. Use the correct form of the present perfect and *ever* or *never*.

1 A: ..*Have*.. you ..*ever seen*.. the Eiffel Tower? (ever/see)

B: No, I ..*'ve never been*.. to France. (never/be)

2 A: .... you .... scuba diving? (ever/try)

B: No, I .... in the ocean. (never/swim)

3 A: .... you .... English to someone who was British? (ever/speak)

B: No, I .... anyone who was British. (never/meet)

4 A: .... you .... to New York? (ever/fly)

B: No, I .... in a plane. (never/be)

5 A: .... you .... awake for 24 hours? (ever/stay)

B: No, and I .... for 24 hours! (never/sleep)

6 A: I .... Japanese food. (never/eat)

B: So, you .... sushi? (never/try)

8 Vocabulary review

✱ Adjectives for feelings and opinions

a Underline the correct choice.

1 The book was so *interesting / boring* that he read it three times.

2 I didn't enjoy the movie last night. It was very *fantastic / dull*.

3 I don't like that painting at all. I think it's really *attractive / ugly*.

4 Those sunglasses are great. You look really *awful / cool* in them!

5 Next week, we're going to Florida on vacation. We're all very *excited / exciting*.

6 I told him all about myself, but I don't think he was *interested / interesting* in listening.

✱ Personality adjectives

b Complete the list of adjectives. Write the opposite of each word.

Positive	Negative
........*friendly*........	unfriendly
organized	
kind	
	dishonest
....	lazy
....	
polite	
	miserable
....	
relaxed	

c Complete the sentences with an adjective from Exercise 8b. The missing word begins with the first letter of each person's name!

1 Ursula never says hello when she sees you on the street. She's very ..*unfriendly*.. .

2 Robbie never gets nervous before a test. He's always ....

3 Lucy never does any work. She's very ....

4 Peggy's very .... She always says please and thank you.

5 Mike's feeling .... today. He had an argument with his father.

6 Don't believe anything that Debbie says. She's very ....

7 Dave is really .... There are papers everywhere on his desk!

8 Everybody likes Frank. He's very ....

Where's my cell phone?

9 Read and listen

a ▶ CD1 T10 Look at the photo story. What did Matt get for his birthday? What happened to it? What was Alex's idea? Read and listen to find the answers.

1

Matt: You won't believe what my parents gave me for my birthday!

Kim: Uh, let's see, a motorcycle?

Matt: Ha! Ha! Very funny. No, it's one of those new cell phones. It does all kinds of stuff.

Alex: Cool. Can we see it?

2

Matt: Sure. Here it … Oh no, I've lost it! It was in my pocket.

Emily: OK. Don't panic. Are you sure it was in your pocket?

Matt: Yes, I put it there when I left the house.

Kim: And where did you go after that?

3

Matt: Well, I went to the library to get a book for school.

Alex: Great! Let's go and look for it there.

Matt: But I was all over the library. We'll never find it.

Alex: Sure, we will. You'll see.

4

Kim: Now think. Exactly where did you go?

Matt: Let's see. First, I went to the computers to look up a book.

Emily: Alex, what are you doing? You can't use your cell phone in here.

Alex: Wait just a minute. Listen! [*Sfx cell phone ringing.*]

Matt: That's my phone! There it is, by the computers! Alex, you're a genius.

Kim and Emily: Shhh!

b Number the sentences in the correct order.

.... Matt put his phone in his pocket.

.... Alex made a call on his cell phone.

.... Matt found his cell phone.

.... Matt went to the library to get a book.

....*1*.... Matt's parents gave him a cell phone for his birthday.

.... Matt told his friends he lost his cell phone.

.... Kim, Alex, Emily and Matt went to the library.

.... Matt looked up a book on the computer at the library.

10 Everyday English

a Find expressions 1–6 in the story. Who says them? Write *Kim*, *Alex*, *Emily* or *Matt*.

1 Let's see. ....
2 You won't believe ....
3 Don't panic. ....
4 all over ....
5 Just a minute. ....
6 You'll see. ....

b Complete the sentences with the expressions in Exercise 10a.

1 .... , but there's a small fire in the library. We need to leave the building now!

2 I went .... the house looking for my math book, but I couldn't find it.

3 A: Bill, would you please help me with these boxes?

   B: .... I'll be right there.

4 A: .... what I just heard in the cafeteria!

   B: What? Tell me!

5 A: How are you going to get your mom to let you go?

   B: .... I have an idea!

6 A: What do think we should get Dad for his birthday?

   B: Hmm. .... How about that new book he wants?

Discussion box

1 What do you usually do when you lose something? How do you try to find it?

2 Tell about a time when you lost something. Did you find it? If not, how did you feel about it?

11 Improvisation

Work with a partner. Take two minutes to prepare a short role play. Try to use some of the expressions from Exercise 10a. Do not write the text, just agree on your ideas for a short scene. Then act it out.

Basic idea: Imagine that Matt didn't find his cell phone. He's explaining to his mom or dad what happened.

12 Step Up ⦿ DVD Episode 1

a Match the words and expressions with the definitions.

..........g.......... 1 down
.... 2 I guess not.
.... 3 drop out (of school)
.... 4 What's up?
.... 5 upset
.... 6 bummer
.... 7 Hang on!
.... 8 fridge

a What's happening?
b refrigerator
c worried, unhappy
d bad news, something disappointing (informal)
e leave, stop doing something
f I don't think so.
g sad, depressed
h Wait! Don't give up.

b How do you feel when you have to go back to school after a long vacation? What do you have to do to get ready?

c Look at the photo. Emily, Kim, Alex and Matt are getting ready for another year of school. How do you think they feel? Why? Is it just that they're going back to school, or do they have some other problem? Watch Episode 1 and find out.

13 Write

a Alan had to write an essay for his English class about what he did during his vacation and what he learned from it. Read the paragraphs from Alan's essay. They are in the wrong order. Number them 1–3 in the correct order.

Learning on the job

.... I worked from 6 a.m. to 2 p.m., from Tuesday to Saturday. First, I had to unpack boxes of food when the trucks delivered them. Then, I had to check everything and make sure it was in good condition. If there was a problem with a product, we sent it back. After that, I put the things on the shelves. I marked everything with the correct price. For this, I used a scanner that was connected to the store's computer. During the day, I checked the shelves to make sure they weren't empty. Shoppers don't like to see empty shelves in the store!

.... I learned a lot from this job. Now I understand how stores, like supermarkets, work. I also learned a lot about people. I worked with people of all ages and from many different places. Finally, the job taught me about being responsible. I had to be on time every day and make sure the food was on the shelves. My job was important for the store's business.

.... I need to save some money for college, so for this vacation, I decided that I should get a job and make some money. I applied for a job as a stock clerk at a small supermarket near my house. I was lucky. I got the job!

b Read Alan's essay again. Answer the questions.

1 What did Alan do during his vacation?

2 How many hours did he work each day?

3 How did he find the prices for the things he put on the shelves?

4 What did he learn from the job?

c Write an essay about something you did during a vacation and what you learned from it. It can be a job, a trip or any activity you did during the vacation. Use Alan's essay to help you.

14 Last but not least: more speaking

a Read this statement from a local newspaper.

"Residents of the town are saying that school summer vacations are too long. During the vacation, kids forget things and get into trouble. They think that schools should give only two weeks of vacation in the summer."

b Work with a partner. Write three reasons for this idea and three against it. Don't give your own opinions at this time.

Summer vacations are too long.	
For	Against

c Work with another pair. Compare your ideas. Then discuss the question: Are summer vacations too long? Give your own opinions.

Check your progress

1 Grammar

a Choose the correct answer. (Circle) a, b or c.

1 The weather is crazy. Right now it _____ .
   (a) 's raining b rains c rain

2 Yesterday we _____ through snow in the mountains.
   a drive b driving c drove

3 A doctor _____ visit patients in the hospital.
   a don't have to b have to c has to

4 Salespeople _____ have a college degree.
   a don't have to b doesn't have to
   c not have to

5 No, we _____ . We _____ a taxi.
   a does / take b doesn't / 're taking
   c didn't / took

6 I hope there aren't _____ onions in the salad.
   a some b any c no

7 Josh doesn't drink _____ milk. He doesn't like it.
   a much b a c many

8 I have _____ ideas about the problem.
   a some b any c an   [8]

b Underline the correct words in each sentence.

1 We _'ll probably be_ / _won't probably be_ late for school. We just missed the 7 bus.

2 Linda is the _lazy_ / _laziest_ person in our group. She's even _lazier_ / _laziest_ that I am!

3 Try to walk _more quiet_ / _quietly_. The people downstairs have complained about the noise.

4 Your parents _is going to be_ / _are going to be_ very happy when they see your grades.

5 If you _'re_ / _will be_ rude to someone, that person _is_ / _will_ be rude to you.

6 You _should_ / _shouldn't_ get more sleep. Then you won't be so tired all the time.

7 _Have ever you_ / _Have you ever_ heard that story before?   [8]

2 Vocabulary

a (Circle) the word or phrase in each group that is different.

1 doctor dentist (architect)

2 flight attendant lawyer pilot

3 ice cream milk carrots

4 fish apples bananas

5 next month last Saturday the day after tomorrow

6 sun thunder lightning

7 kind mean friendly

8 miserable nervous happy   [7]

b Choose the correct word or phrase for each sentence. (Circle) a or b.

1 Look, I know the job is hard, but don't _____ now. You're almost finished.
   a take up (b) give up

2 Today is Thursday, and the party's on Saturday. That's _____ .
   a next week b the day after tomorrow

3 Our friends will be here _____ . Let's clean the house!
   a after two hours b in two hours

4 Some people don't like rock music, but I think it's very _____ .
   a exciting b excited

5 Our trip to Africa was _____ . We saw all kinds of interesting animals.
   a dull b fantastic

6 They painted the house purple and bright pink! Ugh! It looks _____ .
   a ugly b attractive   [5]

How did you do?

Check your score.

Total score	☺	☹	☹
[28]	Very good	OK	Not very good
Grammar	16 – 13	12 – 10	9 or less
Vocabulary	12 – 10	9 – 8	7 or less

3 Great idea!

* Past continuous
* Past continuous vs. simple past, *when* and *while*
* Vocabulary: *get*

1 Read and listen

a Match the words in the box with the pictures. Write 1–8 in the boxes.

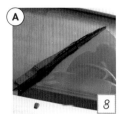
A 8

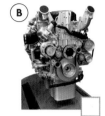
B

C

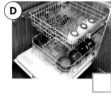
D

E

F

G

H

1 chewing gum
2 remote control
3 roller skates
4 diesel engine
5 mousetrap
6 stove
7 dishwasher
8 ~~windshield wipers~~

b Read the text. What do you think each person invented? Choose from the objects in Exercise 1a.

c ▶ CD1 T11 Listen to the complete stories and check your answers.

d ▶ CD1 T11 Listen again and answer the questions.

1 What happened when Thomas put a piece of chicle in his mouth?
2 What did James Henry Atkinson do with his idea?
3 Who bought Josephine Cochrane's invention first?
4 Why did the Dutchman get impatient?

What did they invent?

In 1902, Mary Anderson and a friend were riding on a streetcar in New York City. It was snowing. Mary noticed that the driver of the streetcar had to drive with the front window open in order to see. Suddenly, Mary had an idea.

In 1869, Thomas Adams was trying to make rubber out of a material called *chicle*, a product of the Mexican sapodilla tree. Adams knew that Mexicans enjoyed chewing chicle, but he wanted to use it to produce rubber for toys, rain boots and bicycle tires. The experiment didn't work. While he was thinking about this, he took a piece of the chicle and put it in his mouth.

In 1897, British inventor James Henry Atkinson was looking at the family's supply of potatoes. The family kept the potatoes in a room under their house. He noticed that mice had eaten some of the potatoes, so he invented something called the "Little Nipper" to stop them.

In 1886, in the state of Illinois, Josephine Cochrane was standing in her kitchen after a big dinner party. She was looking at several broken dishes. Mrs. Cochrane loved to give dinner parties, but cleaning up afterward was a problem. Her servants broke too many dishes. Mrs. Cochrane got very angry and said, "If nobody else is going to invent a machine to do this work, I'll do it myself."

In the early years of the 18th century, in the middle of summer, an unknown Dutchman was looking at one of the many canals in Holland. He was thinking about the fun he had ice-skating on the frozen canals in winter. He got a little impatient. "I don't want to wait for winter," he thought.

2 Grammar

✳ Past continuous

a Look at the examples.

Mary Anderson and a friend were riding on a streetcar …   Josephine Cochrane was standing in her kitchen.

b Underline other examples of the past continuous in the text on page 16.
Then read the rule and complete the table.

Affirmative	Negative	Question	Short answer
I/he/she/it _____ working	I/he/she/it _____ (**was not**) working	_____ I/he/she/it working?	Yes, I/he/she/it _____ . No, I/he/she/it _____ (**was not**).
you/we/they _____ working	you/we/they **weren't** (**were not**) working	_____ you/we/they working?	Yes, you/we/they _____ . No, you/we /they _____ (**were not**).

RULE: Use the past continuous to talk about actions in progress at a certain time in the past.

c Yesterday, Tom's math teacher was late. What were the students doing when she got to the class? Complete the sentences with the past continuous form of the verbs in the box.

write   d̶o̶   sit   play   dream

1 Lucy _was doing_ a handstand.
2 Daniel and Sophie _____ table tennis.
3 Samuel _____ on the teacher's desk.
4 Ken _____ a text message.
5 Lisa _____ about a day on the beach.

d Complete the sentences. Use the past continuous form of the verbs.

1 A: What _were you doing_ (you/do) when I saw you yesterday?
   B: I _____ (wait) for my sister. She _____ (buy) something in a store.
2 A: Who _____ (you/talk) to when I called you?
   B: It was my brother. He _____ (tell) me about a movie he saw on TV.
3 A: _____ (his parents/live) in the U.S. when he was born?
   B: No, they _____ (live) in Paris. His father _____ (work) as an architect.
4 A: _____ (you/watch) TV when I called last night?
   B: No, I wasn't. I _____ (read) a magazine.
5 A: Who _____ (you/have) lunch with when I saw you yesterday?
   B: With Jane. She's a friend of mine. We _____ (talk) about you!
6 A: _____ (you/play) tennis yesterday afternoon?
   B: No, I _____ (not/play) tennis, I _____ (do) my homework.
7 A: What _____ (they/wear) yesterday? Their school uniform?
   B: No, they _____ (not/wear) their school uniform, they _____ (wear) jeans and T-shirts.

 3 **Pronunciation**

▶ **CD1 T12 and T13** Pronunciation section starts on page 114.

 4 **Speak**

Work in groups. One of you is a famous person. The others ask questions to find out what he/she was doing at a certain time in the past. The "star" invents the answers.

Q: *What **were** you **doing** last Sunday at 7 p.m.?*

A: *Oh, I was on a plane. I **was flying** from … to …*

Q: *Who was with you?*

A: *My assistant and some reporters.*

Q: *What **were** you **doing** during the flight?*

A: *I **was talking** to the reporters. And I **was writing** some emails.*

Q: *Were you …?*

5 Listen

a Read the beginning of a science fiction story and answer the questions.

1 Who or what was in the spaceships?
2 What do you think happened after the spaceship landed?
3 What do you think happened after Olivia finished writing her story?

b ▶ **CD1 T14** Listen to the rest of the story. Check your ideas from Exercise 5a.

c What do you think happened in the end?

Olivia's story

Olivia was sitting at her desk, writing a story. It was about a far away planet, XR017. Many people were living on the planet. There wasn't enough space for everyone, so the president of XR017 sent five spaceships to find out more about Earth. As they were getting near Earth, four of the spaceships caught on fire. Only one of them got to Earth and landed safely. In it was ....

6 Grammar

✳ Past continuous vs. simple past

a Look at this sentence from the story. Underline the past continuous verb and ⊙circle the simple past verb.

As they were getting near Earth, four of the spaceships caught fire.

b Look at the diagram. Which sentence tells us the background action? Which sentence tells us what happened at one moment? Complete the rule.

*As they **were getting** near Earth* ⟶

↑

*four of the spaceships **caught** fire.*

> **RULE:** Use the .... for a background action or description.
> Use the .... for an action that happened at one particular moment.

c Look at the sentences from the story. Complete them with the correct form of the verbs.

1 While he *was working* (work) on his plan, his brain machine .... (check) people's brains to find out what they .... (think).
2 Every now and then, Q5 .... (look) at the huge screen. Everything .... (go) well. All the human brains .... (think) of other things, and none of them .... (know) about his terrible plans.
3 When Olivia .... (look) at the neighbor, she .... (see) that he .... (hold) something in his hand. It looked like a cell phone.

✳ *when* and *while*

d Look at these sentences from the story. Then complete the rule.

*Olivia was writing the last sentence of her story, **when** suddenly she **heard** a noise behind her.*

***While** he **was smiling**, he got a shock.*

> **RULE:** We often use *when* with the .... past and *while* with the past ....

e Complete the sentences. Put one of the verbs into the simple past, and one into the past continuous.

1 I *was writing* (write) an email. The phone *rang* (ring).
2 Harry .... (run) to school. He .... (fall) and hurt his leg.
3 Alex and Sue .... (play) tennis. Lucy .... (arrive).
4 Antonio .... (have) breakfast. He .... (have) a great idea.

f Combine the sentences in Exercise 6e in two different ways. Use *when* and *while*.

*I was writing an email **when** the phone rang.*

***While** I was writing an email, the phone rang.*

 **Read**

a Try to answer the following questions. Then read through the text quickly to find the answers.

1 What did the Wright brothers invent?

2 Do inventions always come from older people?

Be an inventor!

The biggest secret about inventing is that anybody can do it! Perhaps this sounds crazy, but it's true. Maybe you have the wrong idea about inventing, so read on to discover the truth.

**Wrong idea number 1:
An invention has to be something completely new.**

Well, inventing means creating something "new," but the idea could come from something that already exists. The Wright brothers, for example, got the idea for building a "flying machine" from watching birds.

**Wrong idea number 2:
Inventors are born, not made.**

There are a lot of factors that make innovation possible. Take Mozart, for example. He was born with a unique talent for musical composition. But other factors were also important for his creativity. His father was a music teacher, and Mozart practiced for hours every day, from the time he was four years old.

Thomas Edison said that being an inventor was "99% hard work and 1% inspiration"!

Very successful creators don't give up when they get something wrong. As one inventor said, "A failure is the right answer to the wrong question."

**Wrong idea number 3:
Inventors are always old people.**

Don't believe that you can't invent something when you are young. Here are two examples of young inventors:

Louis Braille went blind when he was a child. When he was 15, he invented a system of reading and writing for blind people that is still used in most countries today.

As a young man, George Nissen was watching trapeze artists in a circus. He watched how they fell into the safety net and then bounced back up again. This gave him an idea, and he invented the trampoline.

b Read the text and match the two parts of the sentences.

1 Many people don't know that

2 The Wright brothers got the idea for

3 Many inventors have a lot of talent,

4 If you give up easily when you

a but they also work very hard.

b make a mistake, you won't be successful.

c anybody can be an inventor.

d building an airplane from watching birds.

c Discuss in groups.

1 Do you agree that "inventing is something anybody can do"? Why / Why not?

2 "Practice makes perfect" is a famous saying. Do you agree?

3 Think of a useful invention. Tell the group about it. Do they think it's useful?

---

8 Vocabulary

★ *get*

a The verb *get* can mean *arrive, receive* or *become*. Look at these sentences. Write the meaning of *got* in each sentence.

He got a little impatient. = ___*became*___

The Wright brothers got the idea for building a flying machine from watching birds. = _____

Only one of the spaceships got to the Earth. = _____

Thomas Adams got the chicle from Mexican sapodilla trees. = _____

LOOK!

Only one spaceship **got to** Earth.
I **got home** at nine o'clock.
(not: I got to home.)

b Complete the sentences with the words in the box. Use the simple past or past continuous forms.

get wet   get to school
~~get the answer~~   get angry

1 The math question was very hard, but in the end I __*got the answer*__ .

2 I woke up at 8:30 this morning, so I _____ really late.

3 Alex stopped playing football because it was raining and he _____ .

4 My teacher _____ because I didn't do my homework.

Culture in mind

9 Read and listen

a In pairs ask and answer questions.

1 Do you like listening to music? Why / Why not?

2 How do you most often listen to music: on the radio, a CD player or an MP3 player?

b Read the article and choose the best title for it.

1 Isn't music wonderful?

2 The history of listening to music

3 Listening to music 100 years ago

c ▶ CD1 T15 Read the article again and listen. Answer the questions.

1 When did families stop using player pianos? Why?

2 What was the problem with the first records?

3 What was the main difference between phonographs and gramophones?

4 What did people like about portable cassette players?

People all over the world love listening to music, and most have their favorite songs that they listen to again and again. But how did it all start? When could people first choose the music they wanted to listen to?

The 1900s: The player piano

In the late 19th and early 20th centuries, pianos became very popular and rich families bought "player pianos." A player piano plays music that is programmed on paper rolls with holes in them. You can also play it like a "normal" piano. In the mid 1920s, player pianos began to disappear, mainly because the radio (it was called the wireless in those days) got more popular.

The 1910s: The first phonographs

As early as 1877, there were phonographs to play music on and, by the 1910s, many families had one. The music was on "records" made of aluminum foil. People could listen to them only a few times before the foil broke. Later, the music was on wax cylinders. These could hold longer recordings (two to four minutes), and people could play them more often.

1920–1940s: Gramophones and record players

Gramophones were similar to the phonographs, but they used flat vinyl disks and not cylinders to hold the music. The disks spun around, and first a steel needle, then later a small diamond, "took" the music off the record. Some music specialists and disc jockeys still use vinyl records today.

The 1960s onward: cassettes and the Walkman

In the 1960s, the first cassette recorders became popular. A big step toward modern technology was the invention of the first portable cassette player, the "Walkman," by the Japanese company Sony in 1979. For the first time, people could listen to their favorite music while they were traveling, playing sports or going for walks.

d Find words in the text that mean:

1 that many people like (paragraph 2)
2 not be seen (any more) (paragraph 2)
3 not many times (paragraph 3)
4 not very different from (paragraph 4)
5 a person playing music on the radio or in a disco (paragraph 4)

You probably know the rest of the story. You know what audio CDs, MP3 and MP4 players are. But do you know what will come next?

10 Speak

Discuss in groups.

1 Some people pay a lot of money to buy an old gramophone or record player. Would you do that too? Why / Why not?
2 What will listening to music be like in the future? Make five serious or fun suggestions.

11 Write

a Read Alex's story in Exercise 11b about an invention and answer questions 1–3.

1 What's the name of the invention and who invented it? ☐
2 Why is it a good invention? ☐
3 When and how did the inventor get the idea? ☐

b Match the questions in Exercise 11a with the paragraphs. Write A, B and C in the boxes.

A I'm going to write about the tape called Velcro™. The man who invented it was George de Mestral, from Switzerland.

B De Mestral got the idea in 1948. One day, when he was walking in the woods, he got annoyed because there were a lot of burrs (from plants) on his coat and pants, and it was very difficult to get them off. De Mestral noticed how the burrs were sticking to his clothes, and he used the idea to make a kind of tape out of cotton. He started a factory to make Velcro™ in 1952.

C I think Velcro™ is very useful for things like sneakers and other clothes and also for bags, because it's easy and quick to use.

c Underline the following expressions in Alex's text:

I'm going to write about …
The man who invented it was …
… got the idea …
… noticed …
… started a factory …
I think … is useful because …

d Write a story about an invention. Use Alex's story and the expressions in Exercise 11c to help you.

4 He ran faster.

* Comparative and superlative adjectives
* Intensifiers with comparatives
* (not) as ... as

* Adverbs / comparative adverbs
* Vocabulary: antonyms/sports

1 Listen

a Match the names of the sports events with the pictures. Write 1–6 in the boxes.

1 throwing the discus
2 gymnastics
3 throwing the javelin
4 archery
5 volleyball
6 sprinting

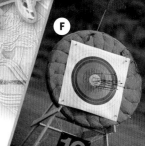
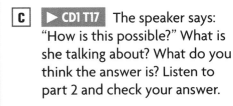

b ▶ CD1 T16 Look at the profiles. Listen to part 1 of a talk and complete the information.

Olympic medalists (Beijing 2008)

Lucas Prado
From: Brazil
Event: _____
Medal: Gold
Time: _____

Christina Obergföll
From: _____
Event: Javelin throw
Medal: _____
Distance: _____

Usain Bolt
From: _____
Event: 200-meter sprint
Medal: _____
Time: 19.30 seconds

Jeny Velazco
From: _____
Event: _____
Medal: Bronze
Distance: _____

c ▶ CD1 T17 The speaker says: "How is this possible?" What is she talking about? What do you think the answer is? Listen to part 2 and check your answer.

d ▶ CD1 T17 Listen to part 2 again and answer the questions.

1 What are the Paralympics?
2 When were the first Paralympic Games?
3 How many athletes were at the 2008 Paralympic Games?
4 Where did Natalie Du Toit finish in the 10 km swim in the Olympics?
5 What is Du Toit's disability?

e Can you think of any other famous disabled people? Tell the class about them.

2 Grammar

✱ Comparative and superlative adjectives

a Complete these sentences from Exercise 1b on page 22. Use the words in the box.

best ~~fastest~~ shorter slower

1 Bolt was the _fastest_ runner.
2 Prado was _____ than Bolt.
3 Velazco's throw was _____ than Obergföll's.
4 Obergföll made the _____ throw.

b Put the adjectives in the box below in the correct columns. How do you form the comparative and superlative of *good* and *bad*?

~~easy~~ bad neat ~~young~~ fast quiet interesting
~~beautiful~~ heavy new expensive ~~good~~

-er/-est	-ier/-iest	more/most	Irregular comparatives
young	_easy_	_beautiful_	_good_

✱ Intensifiers with comparatives

Nick's **much / a lot older** than Will.

The red bike is **a little more expensive** than the green one.

c Compare the things in the sentences. Use *much / a lot* or *a little*.

1 watching TV / reading a book (interesting/easy)
I think watching TV is a lot more interesting than reading a book – and it's easier, too.
2 a cell phone / an MP4 player (useful/expensive)
3 girls / boys (intelligent/neat)
4 history / math (difficult/interesting)
5 my best friend / me (tall/young)
6 my country / the United States (big/beautiful)

3 Vocabulary and grammar

✱ Antonyms

a Match adjectives 1–10 with their opposites in Exercise 2b. How do you form the comparative and superlative?

1 bad _good_
2 difficult _____
3 slow _____
4 boring _____
5 cheap _____
6 light _____
7 noisy _____
8 messy _____
9 ugly _____
10 old _____ / _____

✱ (*not*) *as ... as*

b We can use (*not*) *as ... as* to compare things. Look at the examples. Answer the questions.

*Prado isn't **as fast as** Bolt. Velazco's medal was **as good as** Obergföll's.*

1 Who is faster, Prado or Bolt?
2 Was Velazco's medal better than Obergföll's medal?

c Complete the second sentence so it means the same as the first.

1 Sarah's brother is younger than Sarah. *Sarah's brother isn't _as old as_ her.*
2 Peter's neater than his sister. *Peter isn't _____ his sister.*
3 Traveling by train is faster than traveling by bus. *Traveling by train isn't _____ traveling by bus.*
4 Dogs are noisier than cats. *Dogs aren't _____ cats.*

4 Pronunciation

 CD1 T18 Pronunciation section starts on page 114.

5 Read

a Look at the photo and the title. What is the sport? Who are the teams? Who do you think won? Read the text quickly to check your ideas.

b Read the text again and answer the questions.

1 What was the score at the end of the game?

2 What was the situation after three periods?

3 What did one of the players say about the Australian and Canadian teams?

4 How does the Australian coach feel about the next Paralympic Games?

Australia: Almost the champions

The Australian Men's Wheelchair Basketball team was only two points away from winning a gold medal last night. In the Paralympic Wheelchair Basketball final, Canada (the world and Paralympic champions) beat Australia 49 to 47.

At the end of the third period, Australia was winning by eight points. But Canada came back. The team played very well and took the lead in the last 30 seconds. The Australian captain had a chance at the very end to tie the game, but the ball hit the basket and didn't go in. The referee blew the final whistle and Canada was the champion.

One of the Australian players said: "We're very proud. We didn't play badly. In fact, we played very well. But congratulations to Canada. They played hard and fast and, in the end, they played better than us."

The Australian team now has a few weeks before their next game, but the players aren't resting. They are already preparing for the next Paralympic Games. "We hope that we can go further than last time and win the gold medal," the coach said. "We're practicing even more regularly and we're training harder than ever. I think we'll do very well at the next Paralympics."

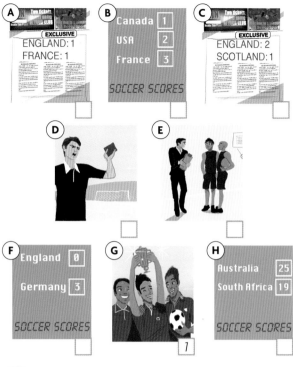

6 Vocabulary

✱ Sports

a Match the sentences with the pictures.

1 They're the **champions**.

2 England **won**, two–one.

3 England **lost**, three–**zero**.

4 It was a **tie**.

5 Australia **beat** South Africa.

6 The U.S. **came in second**.

7 The **coach** talked to the **players**.

8 The **referee ejected** a player.

b Put the pictures into words.

1 _Jones came in first, Smith ..._

2 ....

3 ....

4 ....

7 Grammar

✷ Adverbs / comparative adverbs

a Look at the example. <u>Underline</u> other examples of adverbs in the text on page 24.

*We didn't play **badly**. In fact we played very **well**.*

b How do you form the adverbs of:

- regular adjectives (for example, *slow*)?
- adjectives ending in *-y* (for example, *easy*)?
- *hard*, *fast* and *good*?

LOOK!

We use adjectives to talk about nouns: *He's a **slow runner**.*
We use adverbs to talk about verbs: *He **runs slowly**.*

c Read Mark's diary. (Circle) the correct words.

> May 4
>
> Last night, my father was talking about languages. He says he speaks French ¹good / well, but he doesn't. I've heard him speaking French: He tries to speak very ²quick / quickly, and his pronunciation is ³terrible / terribly. But I didn't say that.
>
> I want to speak Italian ⁴fluent / fluently. Yesterday I talked to the Italian teacher about my test. She said I got 4 out of 20. I did really ⁵bad / badly on the test. I was surprised. I thought the test was ⁶easy / easily and I answered all the questions really ⁷quick / quickly.
>
> The teacher said I'll never be ⁸good / well at Italian, but I smiled ⁹happy / happily at her because she's wrong. I'm going to learn Italian and go to live in Rome.

d Look at this example of a comparative adverb from the text on page 24. Then complete the rule.

*We're practicing even **more regularly** ....*

> **RULE:** To form the comparative of most regular adverbs, add the word _____ before the adverb.

e Some comparative adverbs add *-er/-ier* to the adverb, others change completely. Complete the examples.

1 soon   *sooner*   4 hard   _____
2 early   *earlier*   5 fast   _____
3 good   _____   6 bad   _____

f Complete the sentences. Write the comparative adverbs of the adjectives.

1 Sue runs _*faster*_ (fast) than me.

2 Andy writes _____ (clear) than me.

3 Pablo speaks English _____ (fluent) than me.

4 Sorry, I don't understand. Can you speak _____ (slow), please?

5 I got 90% on the test, but Jeff did even _____ (good) than me.

6 Rebecca ran _____ (quick) than Alice.

7 Sandra always works _____ (hard) than everyone else.

8 The party starts at 9:00, but you can come _____ (early) if you want to.

8 Speak

a Think of five famous people, or people in your class, and compare how they do things. Start each sentence with "He" or "She." Use the verbs and adjectives in the box.

> play   speak   work   sing
> dance   run   write   learn
> act [your ideas]
>
> good   hard   bad   clear
> fluent   quick [your ideas]

He plays tennis better than Rafael Nadal.

She works harder than anyone else in the class.

b In pairs, tell each other your sentences. Who is your partner thinking of?

A marathon

9 Read and listen

a ▶ CD1 T19 Look at the photostory. Someone is taking part in a sports event. Who is it? What is the event? Why is Alex laughing in picture 2? Read and listen to find the answers.

Alex: You're not going to believe this. My mom's running in this!

Kim: Your mom? In a marathon? I didn't know she liked running.

Alex: Well, she doesn't really. She runs a little now and then, and she goes to the gym, you know, that kind of thing. But there's no way she can finish a marathon.

Three days later

Matt: So, Alex, how did your mom do?

Alex: Ha, ha, ha! It took her 7 hours and 12 minutes.

Emily: So, she finished the marathon? That's fantastic!

Alex: Yeah, but guess what? She was one of the slowest runners in the race!

Matt: Still. We're talking about 42 kilometers here. That's an awful lot of running. There's no way I could do that.

Kim: It would take me more than a month. And honestly, Alex, do you think you could do it?

Alex: That's not the point. It took her more than 7 hours. It's so embarrassing!

Emily: So what? She set herself a goal, and she did it. At the end of the day, that's what matters.

Alex: Well, maybe you're right. I've never thought about it like that, I suppose.

b Read the sentences. Find one thing that's wrong in each sentence and correct it.

1 Alex thinks his mom is enthusiastic about sports.
2 Alex's mom finished the marathon, and Alex was impressed with her time.
3 No other runner was slower than Alex's mom.
4 Matt thinks he is a better runner than Alex's mom.
5 Kim and Matt think it's ridiculous to run a marathon in seven hours.

10 Everyday English

a Find the expressions 1–6 in the story. Who says them?

1. ... that kind of thing.
2. Guess what?
3. We're talking about ...
4. ... an awful lot of ...
5. That's not the point.
6. At the end of the day, ...

b Complete the dialogue with the phrases 1–6 in Exercise 10a.

Allie: Hey, Steve. [1] _Guess what?_ I just saw a new Coldplay DVD in the store. It costs $40.

Steve: Really? Well, I'm not going to buy it.

Allie: What!? Steve, [2] _____ Coldplay here – one of your favorite bands!

Steve: I know. But [3] _____ , Allie. Don't you remember? My father lost his job. I can't spend money on CDs, DVDs and [4] _____ .
[5] _____ $40 is
[6] _____ money.

Allie: Oh, yes, I'm sorry. I forgot.

Discussion box

1. Why do you think Alex laughs when he tells his friends about his mother's finishing time?
2. Do you agree with Emily that what is important is to set yourself a goal and go for it? Why / Why not?
3. Is there any sport or other activity that you enjoy doing without being very good at it?

---

11 Improvisation

Work with a partner. Take two minutes to prepare a short role play. Try to use some of the expressions from Exercise 10a. Do not write the text, just agree on your ideas for a short scene. Then act it out.

Basic idea: It's the evening of the same day. Alex is talking to his mom. He's sorry that he made fun of his mom's marathon time.

---

12 Step Up ⊙ DVD Episode 2

a Emily, Kim, Matt and Alex are starting another year of high school. In one of their classes, Alex has to do a special project. What do you think the project is, and how does Alex like it?

b Match the words with their definitions. Then watch Episode 2.

1. drama
2. workshop
3. grade
4. bunch
5. complain about something
6. grumpy
7. talented
8. improvise

a. a number or letter that shows how good you are in a subject at school
b. in a bad mood; unhappy with everything
c. a group of people or things
d. showing a special ability to do something
e. a meeting of people to train or discuss an activity
f. when acting, to make up things
g. to say that something is wrong or you are not happy with it
h. a play in a theater, on TV or on the radio

13 Write

a Marty's teacher asked him to write a report about a sports event. Read Marty's report and answer the questions.

1 What kind of event was it?

2 When and where was it?

3 How did the teams and players play?

4 Who scored the goals for Newton?

5 What was the final score?

6 Did Marty have a good time? Why / Why not?

b Read Marty's report again and match the topics 1–3 with the paragraphs. Write A, B and C in the boxes.

1 What happened at the event ☐

2 Marty's opinion of the event ☐

3 General information about the event ☐

A Last Saturday afternoon, my dad and I went to a soccer game. My high school, Newton High School, was playing the team from Greenville High School. They played here at Newton.

B The game was really exciting from the start. Greenville scored a goal in the first ten minutes of the game. They were playing very well. But after half time, the Newton team started to play better. Mario Vargas, one of our best players, was excellent. After 60 minutes, he scored a goal. Then ten minutes later, he scored another one. So we were winning 2-1. But five minutes before the end, Greenville scored again. The game ended in a tie. The score was 2-2. I was happy because our team didn't lose.

C I think it was a fantastic game because both teams played well. The game was exciting up to the very end. My dad really enjoyed watching Mario Vargas play. After the game, we went out for pizza. It was a great afternoon.

c Write a report for your school magazine about a sports event you watched in the past. Use Marty's report and the questions in Exercise 13a to help you.

14 Last but not least: more speaking

a Look at column A. Make Yes/No questions.

A: Question 1	B: Name	C: Question 2
1 you / watch sports on TV? *Do you watch sports on TV?*	....	What / watch? *What do you watch?*
2 you / play any sports?	....	What / play?
3 you / have a favorite athlete?	....	Who / be?
4 your parents / like sports?	....	What / like?
5 anyone in your family / play a sport well?	....	Who....? What / play?

b Make more questions with the words in column C.

c Ask other students the questions in A. If the answer is yes, write his/her name in column B. Then ask the questions in column C.

d Now work in pairs. Tell your partner about the students you talked to.

Check your progress

1 Grammar

a Complete the sentences. Use the simple past or past continuous form of the verbs.

While I *was walking* (walk) down the street yesterday, I [1]_____ (see) a friend of mine. He [2]_____ (look) in a store window. I [3]_____ (start) to cross the street to say hello to him. While I [4]_____ (cross) the street, I [5]_____ (hear) a noise. A bus [6]_____ (come) in my direction! The bus [7]_____ (stop) very close to me. I was lucky it [8]_____ (not hit) me!

| 8 |

b Complete the sentences.
Use the comparative or superlative form of the <u>underlined</u> adjectives

1 I'm a <u>good</u> player, but Steve is *better* than me, and Jane is the *best* player in the school!

2 Question 1 was <u>easy</u>. Question 4 was _____ than question 1, and question 6 was the _____ question of all.

3 Last night's game was <u>exciting</u>, but Saturday's game was _____ than last night's game, and Sunday's game was the _____ ever.

4 Yesterday was a <u>bad</u> day for me, but Thursday was _____ than yesterday, and Friday was the _____ day of my life!

| 6 |

c Complete the sentences. Write the adverbs.

1 They ran home *quickly* . (quick)

2 She smiled _____ . (happy)

3 My brother speaks French _____ . (fluent)

4 The hairdresser cut my hair very _____ . (bad)

5 I answered all the questions _____ . (easy)

6 Our team played very _____ . (good)

| 5 |

2 Vocabulary

a Put the letters in the correct order to find the adjectives and write them next to their opposites.

~~ogod~~   udifticfl   guly   smeys
yonsi   pxsivenee   lows

1 bad   *good*

2 fast   _____

3 cheap   _____

4 beautiful _____

5 neat   _____

6 quiet   _____

7 easy   _____

| 6 |

b Complete the sentences. Use the correct form of the verb *get* and one of the words in the box.

home   a surprise   good ideas
the answer   old   ~~wet~~

1 It rained very hard last Saturday when I was downtown, and I *got* very *wet* .

2 Our dog can't walk very well because he's _____ very _____ now.

3 I _____ yesterday. My uncle sent me some money!

4 The party was great, and I didn't _____ until midnight!

5 My brother says he _____ when he daydreams.

6 I love math, and I'm always happy when I _____ right.

| 6 |

How did you do?

Check your score.

Total score	☺	☹	☹
31	Very good	OK	Not very good
Grammar	19 – 15	14 – 12	11 or less
Vocabulary	12 – 10	9 – 8	7 or less

5 Our world

* *will/won't*; *might (not) / may (not)* for prediction
* *if/unless* + first conditional
* Vocabulary: the environment

1 Read and listen

a Look at the photos and the title. How is Paris trying to solve its traffic problems? Read the text and check your ideas.

BICYCLE REVOLUTION?

1 Like all big cities, Paris has a traffic problem: a lot of cars, a lot of traffic jams and a lot of pollution from exhaust fumes. So in 2007, the city developed a plan to improve the situation.

Under the Velib program ("Velib" comes from *vélo liberté*, or "bicycle freedom"), people can take a bicycle, use it for as long as they want, and then leave it at the same or another bicycle station. The first half hour on the bike is free, but if you don't return it after 30 minutes, you have to pay. But it's only 1 euro a day or 29 euros a year! The bicycles are heavy (25 kg), and they are all gray and have baskets. There are about 20,000 of them in the city, and around 1,450 bicycle stations. So there are a lot more Velib stations than the 298 metro stations!

2 Paris is not the first city to have a program like this – not even in France, where Lyon started a free bicycle program many years ago. And not everybody thinks it's a great idea. One Parisian said, "These bicycles are only for short trips. If people want to travel across the city, they won't use a bicycle. They'll still use their cars."

3 A city spokesman said, "The bicycle program won't solve all our traffic problems, of course. Also bicycle programs often have problems. The bikes are expensive, and it costs money to keep them in good condition. Unfortunately, some people might try to steal them. But if we succeed, the bike program will help reduce pollution in the city and help with the world's problems of global warming and climate change. Some say that the bikes won't do enough. They say that fumes from factories and the loss of the rain forests are more serious causes of global warming. This may be true. But we have to do what we can. There aren't any simple answers to traffic problems and pollution in cities. But unless we do something now, there will be more traffic jams and temperatures will continue to rise, so the problems in our environment will get worse."

b ▶ **CD1 T20** Read the text again and listen. Match the two parts of the sentences.

1 In 2007, politicians in Paris
2 People only have to pay
3 At more than 1,450 bicycle stations,
4 Some people
5 Politicians think the Velib program
6 If we don't change the situation,

a if they use the bike for more than half an hour.
b will still use cars to travel across the city.
c might help to make the air in Paris cleaner.
d people can take bikes and leave them.
e the problem of pollution will get bigger.
f developed a plan to reduce pollution in the city.

c Discuss in groups.

1 What do you think of the idea of bicycle programs for big cities?
2 Are there any programs to reduce pollution in your city/town?

② Vocabulary

✳ The environment

a What do the <u>underlined</u> words from the text on page 30 mean?

(paragraph 1)

1 a lot of cars, a lot of <u>traffic jams</u> and a lot of <u>pollution</u> from <u>exhaust fumes</u>

(paragraph 3)

2 it might <u>reduce pollution levels</u> in the <u>atmosphere</u>

3 <u>factory fumes</u>

4 <u>global warming</u> and <u>climate changes</u>

5 the <u>loss</u> of rain forests

6 temperatures will continue to <u>rise</u>

7 the problems in our <u>environment</u> will get worse

b ▶ **CD1 T21** Match the words with the pictures. Write 1–6 in the boxes. Then listen, check and repeat.

1 recycling	2 litter
3 ~~pollution~~	4 factory fumes
5 rain forests	6 garbage

c Complete the sentences with the verbs in the box.

waste   ~~drop~~   clean up   recycle
pick up   cut down   pollute

1 Don't ___drop___ litter. Someone has to _____ it _____ !

2 We will _____ your empty bottles. Leave them here.

3 Water is important, so don't _____ it.

4 Every year, people have to _____ thousands of tons of oil from beaches.

5 Factories and power stations _____ the air we breathe and our water.

6 Every year, companies _____ 78 million acres of rain forest, an area larger than the state of Texas.

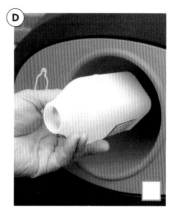

③ Speak

a Work with a partner. Make a list of problems in the environment where you live.

There are a lot of cars, and there is a lot of air pollution.
There is a lot of litter on the streets.

b Put your list in order of how serious you think the problems are. Number 1 is the most serious. Compare your list with other pairs.

c Now make another list of things people can do to improve the environment.

I think we can use bicycles or walk for short trips.
We can recycle our bottles and cans.

d Which of the things in your list do you do now?

4 Grammar

✱ *will/won't*, and *might (not) / may (not)* for prediction

a Look at the examples. <u>Underline</u> other examples of *will/won't* and *might (not) / may (not)* in the text on page 30. Then complete the rule.

They'll still use their cars.
Some people might try to steal them.

> **RULE:** Use _____ or *won't* to express certainty and _____ *(not)* or *may (not)* to express possibility.

b Complete the sentences. Use *will, 'll* or *won't* and the verbs.

1 Great! The weather forecaster on TV says it __will be__ (be) sunny tomorrow.

2 Do you think people in the future _____ (travel) to other planets like Mars?

3 What time _____ we _____ (arrive) in New York tomorrow, do you think?

4 I love those sneakers! When I get my allowance next week, I think I _____ (buy) them.

5 Please can you help me with my homework? I promise it _____ (take) very long.

c Complete the sentences. Use *might* or *might not* and the verbs.

1 Don't give that ice cream to the cat! It __might get__ (get) sick!

2 A: Where's Alicia?
   B: I'm not sure. I think she _____ (be) at her piano lesson.

3 I don't know if this book is a good present for my brother. He _____ (like) it.

4 Don't put that glass there! Someone _____ (break) it.

5 I'm worried about my math test tomorrow. I _____ (pass) it!

6 In the future, people will probably travel in space and they _____ (live) on other planets.

7 I feel awful. I think I _____ (have) the flu.

d Circle the correct words.

1 Don't throw your skis away. You *might / might not* need them later.

2 You don't need to take a sweater. It *will / won't* be cold there.

3 There's a lot of traffic today. We *might / might not* be late for school.

4 Take your umbrella. I'm sure it *will / may* rain soon.

5 I have no definite plans for my vacation, but I *will / might* go to Florida for a few days.

6 A: Do you think Brazil *will / might* win?
   B: They *will / might*, but Venezuela has a very good team, too.

7 Anne is sick, so I'm sure she *may not / won't* go to the party on Saturday.

5 Pronunciation

▶ **CD1 T22** Pronunciation section starts on page 114.

6 Speak

a Work with a partner. Talk about life in the future, 100 years from now. Make predictions. Use *will/won't, might (not) / may (not)* and the topics in the box.

> Travel and transportation   Clothes
> Food   Money   Education and schools
> Sports   Science   Entertainment (TV, movies, etc.)   Books
> _____ [your idea]

A: *I think students will go to school at home with computers.*

B: *Yes, I agree, and there might not be any teachers or schools!*

b Think of your next school year. Make notes of what you think will/might change, and of the things you think will/might not change. Compare your notes with a partner's.

A: *We'll have the same number of English classes every week.*

B: *Yes, but there might not be the same number of students in the class.*

7 Grammar and speaking

✱ First conditional

a Complete this sentence from the text on page 30. Then complete the rule.

If people want to travel across the city, _____

> **RULE:** Condition clause   Result clause
>
> *If +* ____ *simple +* ____ */ won't.*

b Complete the sentences. Use the correct form of the verbs.

1 If I ___*fail*___ (fail) the test, I ___*'ll take*___ (take) it again.

2 If there _____ (be) more cars on the road in the future, there _____ (be) more pollution.

3 If you _____ (see) Maya, _____ you _____ (give) her my message?

4 If pollution _____ (increase), more plants and animals _____ (die).

5 I _____ (not tell) you my secret if you _____ (not come) to Marco's party with me.

6 My parents _____ (be) really angry if they _____ (see) my bedroom!

c Complete the questions. Use the correct form of the verbs.

1 What ___*will*___ you ___*do*___ (do) if the weather ___*is*___ (be) nice this weekend?

2 Where _____ you _____ (go) if you _____ (go) out this weekend?

3 What _____ you _____ (buy) if you _____ (go) shopping this weekend?

4 If you _____ (not go) out this evening, what _____ you _____ (do)?

5 If your teacher _____ (not give) you any homework today, what _____ you _____ (do)?

6 If you _____ (call) a friend tonight, what _____ you _____ (talk about)?

d Work with a partner. Ask and answer the questions in Exercise 6c.

A: *What will you do if the weather's nice this weekend?*

B: *I'm not sure. I might play basketball with Marco.*

e Make sentences about the pictures. Use *If + will/won't, might (not)* or *may (not)*.

If the girl doesn't run, she might not catch the bus. or *She won't catch the bus if she doesn't run.*

✱ *unless* in first conditional sentences

f Look at the example from the text on page 30. Then (circle) the correct answer in the rule.

Unless we do something now, there will be more traffic jams and temperatures will continue to rise.

(The sentence above means: If we don't do something about it now, there will be traffic jams and temperatures will rise.)

> **RULE:** Unless we do something = If we **do /** **don't do** something

g Match the two parts of the sentences.

1 Unless we leave now,

2 We won't understand

3 I won't have any money

4 Unless he studies harder,

5 Nobody will know our secret

a unless my dad gives me some.

b he'll fail his test.

c unless you tell someone.

d we'll be late.

e unless our teacher explains.

Culture in mind

8 Listen

a ▶ CD1 T23 Listen to seven facts about water. Number the pictures 1–7.

Water, water – but it isn't everywhere

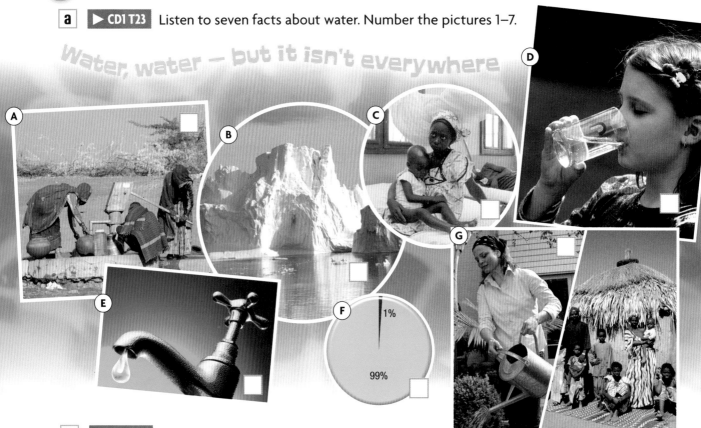

b ▶ CD1 T23 Match. Then listen again and check.

1	99%	a	of the world's diseases are caused by drinking dirty water.
2	70%	b	of the world's fresh water is in places that we cannot get to.
3	500 liters	c	of water are used by one person in the U.S. or Europe every day.
4	20 liters	d	of water are used by an African family every day.
5	88%	e	of all the fresh water in the world is in Antarctica.

c ▶ CD1 T23 What problems do some people in the world have with getting water? Listen again and check your answers.

d ▶ CD1 T24 Guess the answers to these questions. Then listen to an interview with an expert and check your answers.

1 What is the aim of SafeWater?

2 Thirty percent of all the world's fresh water is not frozen in the polar ice caps, but we can still only get to one percent. Where is the rest?

3 How much of the total rainfall ends up in rivers? What about the rest?

4 Why isn't there as much water per person as there was 50 years ago?

9 Speak

Work in small groups. Ask and answer the questions.

1 What do you use water for in your daily life? Make a list.

2 What do people use water for in your town/city?

3 Make a list of five ways in which you could save water.

4 Compare your answers with others in your class.

10 Listen

a ▶ CD1 T25 Complete the song with the words in the box. Then listen and check your answers.

parking lot   museum   apples   dollar
gone   paradise   leave

Big Yellow Taxi

(Joni Mitchell)

They paved [1] _____
And put up a [2] _____
With a pink hotel, a boutique
And a swinging hot spot.

(chorus)
Don't it always seem to go
That you don't know what you've got
Till it's [3] _____ *?*
They paved paradise
And put up a parking lot.

They took all the trees
Put 'em in a tree [4] _____
And they charged the people
A [5] _____ and a half just to see 'em

(chorus)

Hey farmer, farmer
Put away that DDT now.
Give me spots on my [6] _____
But [7] _____ me the birds and
the bees, please!

(chorus)

Late last night
I heard the screen door slam
And a big yellow taxi
Took away my old man.
(chorus)

b People say that this song contains statements about the environment. Which lines give environmental messages, do you think, and what are they?

11 Write

a Amy wrote an article for her school website. How many ideas does she have for making her town better for teenagers? Read Amy's article to find the answers.

A better town for teenagers

(I believe) there are many things that we can do to make life in our town a lot better for teenagers.

First of all, I think that our town needs more bike lanes. A lot of teenagers in my town bike everywhere, but it's very dangerous because there is a lot of traffic. If there are more bike lanes in the future, it will be much safer for us.

Also, I believe that we need more places for teenagers to go. In my opinion, we need more clubs and other places where we can meet. Teenagers won't cause problems in the street if there are more places for us to go to.

In addition, teenagers here need more sports facilities. There are places to play ball games like tennis and basketball, but what about other sports, like skateboarding and rollerblading?

Finally, I'm sure that we'll make the town better if we don't drop litter. Our town will be much better for everyone in the future, if we all do something to help now.

b Underline the words and phrases Amy uses to introduce each idea in her article. (Circle) the words and phrases she uses to give her opinion.

c Write an article like Amy's. Use your ideas from Exercise 9, some of the vocabulary in the unit and Amy's article to help you. Plan your writing. Here is a possible plan:

1 say where you live and what the environmental problems are
2 say what people can do
3 think of a positive ending for your article

6 Holiday or vacation?

* Tag questions
* Present perfect; *just/already/yet*
* Vocabulary: British vs. North American English

1 Read and listen

a How much do you know about the U.S. and Canada? Take the quiz. For each question, circle one answer: a, b or c.

b ▶ CD1 T26 Morgan is going to Canada. He's talking to his Canadian friend Janie. Listen and check your answers to the quiz.

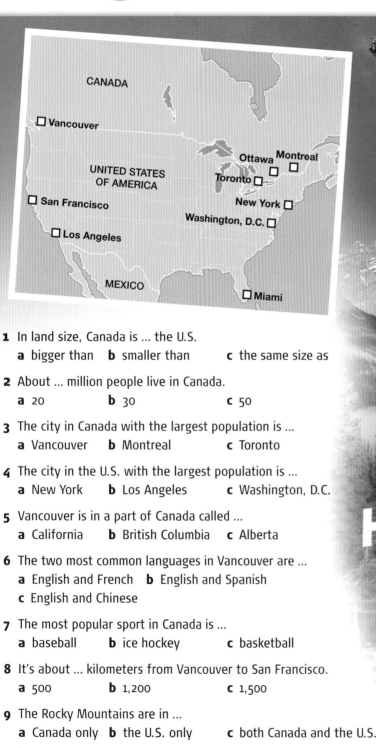

1 In land size, Canada is ... the U.S.
  a bigger than **b** smaller than **c** the same size as

2 About ... million people live in Canada.
  a 20 **b** 30 **c** 50

3 The city in Canada with the largest population is ...
  a Vancouver **b** Montreal **c** Toronto

4 The city in the U.S. with the largest population is ...
  a New York **b** Los Angeles **c** Washington, D.C.

5 Vancouver is in a part of Canada called ...
  a California **b** British Columbia **c** Alberta

6 The two most common languages in Vancouver are ...
  a English and French **b** English and Spanish
  c English and Chinese

7 The most popular sport in Canada is ...
  a baseball **b** ice hockey **c** basketball

8 It's about ... kilometers from Vancouver to San Francisco.
  a 500 **b** 1,200 **c** 1,500

9 The Rocky Mountains are in ...
  a Canada only **b** the U.S. only **c** both Canada and the U.S.

2 Grammar

⭐ Tag questions

a ▶ **CD1 T27** Complete these sentences from the dialogue in Exercise 1b. Then listen to part of Morgan and Janie's conversation again and check your answers.

1 You're Canadian, _aren't_ you?
2 It's smaller than the U.S., _____ it?
3 It isn't Vancouver, _____ it?
4 Cities in the U.S. are much bigger than that, _____ they?
5 You've been there, _____ you?
6 Wow. You don't know much about Canada at all, _____ you?

b All the questions in Exercise 2a have "tags" at the end. "Tags" are short questions that we use to check facts or make conversation. Complete the rule.

> **RULE:** With affirmative statements, we usually use a _negative_ tag question.
> *You're Canadian, **aren't you**?*
>
> With negative statements, we usually use a _____ tag question.
> *It **isn't** Vancouver, **is it**?*
>
> With *be*, modal verbs (*can, must, should, will, might*) and the present perfect, we repeat the auxiliary verb in the tag.
> *You've **been** there, **haven't you**?*
>
> With all other verbs, we use _____ / *does* (simple present) or _____ / *didn't* (simple past).
> *People **speak** French in Canada, too, **don't** they?*

c Match the statements and the tags.

1 He's American,   a isn't it?
2 She doesn't like me,   b do you?
3 She can come with us,   c aren't they?
4 They aren't from Canada,   d do you?
5 They're from the U.S.,   e will she?
6 Your favorite food is pasta, f does she?
7 She won't be at the party,   g can't she?
8 You don't know my sister,   h isn't he?
9 You've been to Italy,   i are they?
10 You don't have a brother,   j haven't you?

d Write the tag questions.

1 He saw us, _didn't he_?
2 They don't live here, _____ ?
3 She likes chocolate, _____ ?
4 You can't come to the party, _____ ?
5 They went to New York, _____ ?
6 She goes to your school, _____ ?
7 You've seen that movie, _____ ?
8 She hasn't done that, _____ ?

3 Pronunciation

▶ **CD1 T28** Pronunciation section starts on page 114.

4 Speak

a Work in groups of four. Ask each other these questions. Don't write the answers!

- What time do you usually go to bed on the weekend?
- What do you usually eat for breakfast?
- What did you have for dinner last night?
- How often do you go to the movies?
- Have you ever been to Chicago?
- Can you walk on your hands?

b Now, try to remember your friends' answers. Use question tags.

Paola, you usually go to bed at 11:00 on the weekend, don't you?

c Work with a partner. Use the words below to make sentences about him/ her that you think are true. Then add tags to make them into questions to ask your partner.

You don't like Chinese food, do you?

- Chinese food
- 14 years old
- basketball
- an apartment
- English
- the U.S.
- sister
- swim

5 Read

a Read the text quickly. Who thinks free Wi-Fi is a good idea? Who thinks it isn't a good idea?

b Read the text again. Write *T* (true) or *F* (false).

1 The city doesn't know yet if the Wi-Fi will be free. ☐

2 Vancouver is the first city to think about free Wi-Fi. ☐

3 In some cities, people pay $10 a month for Wi-Fi. ☐

4 Anna thinks she will want to write emails in her backyard in the future. ☐

5 Anna thinks there is a very good bus system in Vancouver. ☐

6 Tim thinks Vancouver needs more parks. ☐

6 Vocabulary

✲ British vs. North American English

a Match the pictures with the words in the box.

> ~~pants~~ – ~~trousers~~
> lift – elevator
> flat – apartment
> cookies – biscuits
> candy – sweets
> football – soccer
> subway – underground
> lorry – truck
> garbage – rubbish
> sidewalk – pavement

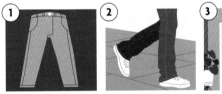
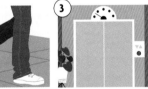
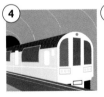

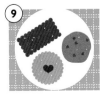

http://www.vancouver.youropinion.cup

VANCOUVER: YOUR OPINION!

Should Vancouver have free wireless internet?

Vancouver is thinking about providing a Wi-Fi network for the downtown area. The city hasn't decided yet, but the network will probably be free.

What do you think of the idea? Post your comment!

It's a good idea, but I'm sure it won't be free. Other cities have already tried it and it hasn't stayed free. Most of them charge about $10 a month. But people are happy to pay because then they can use Wi-Fi in their yards or in Wi-Fi elevators. I've already said this, but I'll say it again: Wi-Fi is a good idea, but I've never heard of a city where it's stayed free for very long.

Comment by Mike (Richmond)

I just read Mike's post. Incredible! I don't want to write emails from an elevator or my yard! I think this is going too far. There are other things the city government could spend the money on, aren't there? For example, more sidewalks or a better bus system.

Comment by Anna (Burnaby)

I agree with Anna. A lot of people have already bought Wi-Fi for their homes. They don't need it on the street, do they?

Spend the money on other things, things for teenagers! The city hasn't built enough schools or parks yet.

Comment by Tim (Ladner)

	Britain	North America
1	trousers	pants
2		
3		
4		
5		
6		
7		
8		
9		
10		

b ▶ CD1 T29 Write the words from Exercise 6a in the correct list. Then listen to Morgan and Janie and check your answers.

7 Grammar

✱ Present perfect, *already* and *yet*

a Look at the examples. <u>Underline</u> other examples of the present perfect in the text on page 38. Then complete the rule.

*A lot of people **have already bought** Wi-Fi for their homes. The city has**n't decided yet**.*

> **RULE:** We form the present perfect with the verb _____ and the _____ form of the main verb.
>
> Use *already* in affirmative sentences. Use *yet* in questions and negatives.
>
> Use *already* between *have* and the _____ . Use _____ at the end of the sentence or question.

b Write the statements and questions. Use the present perfect and *yet* or *already*.

1 A: *Have you seen the new James Bond movie yet?*
   (you / see / the new James Bond movie)

   B: Yes, and _____ . (I / buy / the DVD, too)

2 A: _____ ? (your brother / go / to college)

   B: Yes, and _____ . (I / move / into his old bedroom)

3 A: I love their music, but _____ . (I / not buy / their new CD)

   B: Well, don't buy it! _____ and it's awful. (I / listen to it)

4 A: Paul? _____ ? (you / do / your homework)

   B: Almost. _____ . (I / finish / the math, but I / not start / the geography)

8 Listen

▶ **CD1 T30** Dan is on vacation in New York City. Listen to his conversation with Maggie. Check (✓) the things he has already done. Put an X (✗) next to the things he hasn't done yet.

1 go up the Empire State Building ☐

2 take a ride in a cab ☐

3 ride on the subway ☐

4 see a baseball game ☐

5 eat a hamburger ☐

6 meet any nice American people ☐

7 take a lot of photos of the city ☐

8 buy a present for Maggie ☐

9 Grammar

✱ Present perfect with *just*

a Look at the example. Then complete the rule.

*I'**ve just read** Ken's post.*

> **RULE:** We can use _____ with the present perfect to say that an action happened a very short time ago. Put *just* between _____ and the _____ _____ .

b Use the words to make a sentence with *but* about each picture. Use the present perfect with *just* and *yet*.

1 get a letter / open

   She's just got a letter, but she hasn't opened it yet.

2 go to bed / switch off light

3 buy new bike / ride

4 eat dinner / do the dishes

5 make a fruit smoothie / drink

6 score goal / win

New girl

10 Read and listen

a ▶ CD1 T31 Look at the photostory. There is a new student at school. Where is she from? What do Alex and Matt think about her? Read and listen to find the answers.

1

Matt: Who's that? A new student?

Kim: Yeah, her name's Mi-sun. Her family just moved here from Seoul, South Korea. Her dad has a job with a company in the city.

Matt: Cool! She looks nice.

Alex: Yeah, she does. What do you say we introduce ourselves? Oh, there's the teacher... We have to get to class.

Alex: Mi-sun didn't say a word during the discussion in history class.

Matt: Yeah, I noticed that, too.

Alex: Maybe she didn't understand what we were saying. What do you think?

Kim: Hey, I heard what you guys were saying about Mi-sun.

Matt: Yeah, and so?

Emily: Well, in some cultures, students don't really speak up in class like we do. And besides, she's new and probably a little nervous. No wonder she's quiet.

Alex: Well, maybe, but if she's going to go to school here, she'll have to start talking eventually.

Kim: True, but talking behind her back certainly won't help. Why don't we talk to her?

Emily: Yeah, let's invite her to eat lunch with us.

Kim: Hi, Mi-sun. This is my friend Emily.

Emily: Hi, Mi-sun. So how are things going for you in school?

Mi-sun: Oh pretty good, but everything is so different. Sometimes I don't know what to do.

Kim: Come on and have lunch with us. Maybe we can help.

Mi-sun: That'd be great. Thanks.

b Answer the questions.

1 What do Alex and Matt notice about Mi-sun?

2 What possible reasons does Emily give for this?

3 What do Kim and Emily do to help Mi-sun?

11 Everyday English

a Find the expressions 1–6 in the story. Who says them? How do you say them in your language?

1 What do you say … ?
2 And besides …
3 No wonder …
4 behind (someone's) back …
5 Why don't … ?
6 How are things going … ?

b Complete the dialogues with the phrases 1–6 in Exercise 11a.

1 A: _Why don't_ we work on our project this afternoon?

B: I can't do it today.
   1 .... we do it tomorrow?

2 A: Our teacher had a small accident on the way to school today.

B: Really? 2 .... he looked so upset when he came in.

3 A: 3 .... with the science club?

B: Pretty good. We're planning to have a big science fair next month.

4 A: Did you hear about what Harry did in class today?

B: No, I'm not interested.
   4 .... you shouldn't talk about him 5 .... his ....

Discussion box

1 What do you think about Alex's reaction to Mi-sun in the history class?

2 What do think of the possible reasons that Emily gives? Do you agree?

3 How important is it in your school for students to speak up in class?

---

12 Improvisation

Work with a partner. Take two minutes to prepare a short role play. Try to use some of the expressions from Exercise 11a. Do not write the text, just agree on your ideas for a short scene. Then act it out.

Basic idea: It's the next day. Matt or Emily and Mi-sun are having lunch in the cafeteria. They're talking about how school in the U.S. is different from school in Korea. Matt or Emily gives Mi-sun some advice about what to do in class.

13 Step Up ⊙ DVD Episode 3

a What do you think of the clothing and hair styles of the teens in the picture? Do you like their outfits? Why or why not?

b What do you think Kim, Emily, Alex and Matt would say about their styles?

c Imagine that a friend of yours started to dress in some crazy and very different way. Would that change your relationship? If not, why not? If so, how?

d Some adults react strongly when teenagers wear unusual clothing or hair styles. What do you think of these reactions?

e Watch Episode 3 and find out what happens.

14 Write

a Read the email from Laura to Chris. Answer these questions.

1 Which cities has Laura already visited?

2 Where did she go yesterday, and what did she think of it?

3 Has she visited the Golden Gate Bridge yet?

4 Has she been on a cablecar yet?

5 What has she bought as a present for Chris?

b Now answer these questions.

1 How does Laura begin her email?

2 How does she finish the email?

3 Laura thinks of something more to say after she writes her name. How does she begin this?

c Imagine you are on vacation in a city. Choose one of the cities in the box (or a different city).

New York   Rome
London   Rio de Janeiro
Paris

Write a similar email to an English-speaking friend. Tell him/her what you have and haven't done. Use Laura's email to help you.

Hi, Chris!

How are you? Thanks for your email. I read it yesterday.

So, here I am in California, and I'm in an Internet café in San Francisco, writing to you!

We've had a great time so far. We've been to San Diego and Los Angeles, and San Francisco is the last stop on our vacation. It's a great place and the weather's been beautiful. We've already done a lot of things. Yesterday we went to Alcatraz prison – really interesting! We haven't been to the Golden Gate Bridge yet, but of course I've seen it from the city. Oh, but we've already traveled on one of the famous cablecars here. It was awesome!

Well, it's time for dinner. We've already decided that we're going to eat Mexican tonight. I can't wait!

Hope everything's OK with you. Write again soon, OK?

Love,

Laura

P.S. I've already bought your present – a Giants baseball cap! Hope you like it!

---

15 Last but not least: more speaking

Work in pairs. Student A: Look below. Student B: Turn to page 117.

Student A

a Look at the sentences below. In sentences 1–5, the correct answer is <u>underlined</u>. In sentences 6–10, (circle) what you think is the correct answer.

1 The capital of Canada is *Ottawa* / *Toronto*.

2 The biggest lake in the world is in *Canada and the U.S.* / *Canada*.

3 *Football* / *Basketball* is the most popular sport in the U.S.

4 About *5%* / *10%* of people in the U.S. speak Spanish as their first language.

5 The singers Avril Lavigne and k. d. lang are *Canadian* / *American*.

6 Canada is the *second biggest* / *third biggest* country in the world.

7 There are *50* / *51* states in the U.S.

8 About *200 million* / *300 million* people live in the U.S.

9 Alaska is part of *Canada* / *the U.S.*

10 The singers Mariah Carey and Cher are *Canadian* / *American*.

b Now work with Student B. Check your answers for sentences 6–10. Help Student B check his/her answers for sentences 1–5.

Canada is the second biggest country in the world, isn't it?

Check your progress

1 Grammar

a Complete the sentences with the correct forms of the verbs.

1 If I _clean_ (clean) the house, my parents will _give_ (give) me some extra money.

2 I _____ (call) Mike if he _____ (not arrive) before 10 o'clock.

3 If you _____ (speak) very fast, they _____ (not understand) you.

4 If Marco _____ (call) tonight, _____ you _____ (tell) him I'm at Sally's house?

5 Your parents _____ (not know) if you _____ (not tell) them.

[9]

b Complete the questions with the correct tag questions.

1 You like this music, _don't you_ ?

2 Your sister goes to my school, _____ ?

3 His father's French, _____ ?

4 We're late, _____ ?

5 They aren't at home, _____ ?

6 She hasn't been to Canada, _____ ?

[5]

c Complete the sentences with the correct form of the present perfect.

1 John's _just had_ (just have) his breakfast.

2 A: Would you like some chocolate?
   B: No, thanks. I _____ (already have) some.

3 _____ you _____ (buy) your sister a present yet?

4 We _____ (already finish) our homework.

5 _____ Marta _____ (see) the movie yet?

[4]

2 Vocabulary

a Write the missing British or North American English words.

British English	North American English
flat	1 _apartment_
2 _____	elevator
3 _____	truck
rubbish	4 _____
5 _____	sidewalk

[4]

b Complete clues 1–9 and fill in the puzzle. What's the mystery word?

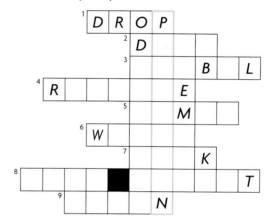

1 Please don't _drop_ litter on the floor.

2 They shouldn't cut _____ those old trees.

3 Temperatures around the world are rising every year. This is called _____ warming.

4 You can _____ glass, paper and plastic.

5 I can't stand the smell of the exhaust _____ from the cars.

6 Please turn off the TV. Don't _____ electricity!

7 There's a lot of litter here on the street. Let's _____ it up.

8 There's a very large _____ in the Amazon.

9 My bike's very dirty, so I'm going to _____ it.

[8]

How did you do?

Check your score.

Total score	☺ Very good	☺ OK	☹ Not very good
[30]			
Grammar	18 – 15	14 – 11	10 or less
Vocabulary	12 – 10	9 – 8	7 or less

7 Growing up

* Present passive
* *let / be allowed to*
* Vocabulary: describing a person's age

Where boys become crocodile men

When does a teenager become an adult? In many countries, it happens on your 18th birthday, but in some parts of the world, you have to do something special to enter the world of adults. On the island of Papua New Guinea, the Niowra tribe lives near the Sepik River, which is full of crocodiles. The people believe that crocodiles made the earth and its people. When it is time for teenage boys to become men, a "crocodile ceremony" takes place.

The boys are taken to a hut called the "Crocodile Nest." The hut is full of crocodile teeth and skulls. The boys are told to think of their crocodile "fathers and mothers." This helps them to be strong and brave during the ceremony. They stay in the hut for six weeks. As part of the ceremony, bamboo is used to make small cuts on their backs and chests. The Niowra say that if the boys think of their crocodile mothers and fathers, they don't feel the pain. The boys also play drums and even tell jokes during their time in the hut to take their minds off the pain. Amazingly, some boys sleep during the most painful parts of the ceremony!

The Niowra believe that this ceremony makes the boys stronger and braver. After the ceremony, the boys will have the marks of the cuts on their backs and chests for the rest of their lives. The marks are symbols of the teeth of the crocodile. The boys are now crocodile men and can survive living in the dangerous forest. When the boys finally leave the crocodile hut, there is singing and dancing, and the new crocodile men are given adult responsibilities in the village.

1 Read and listen

a Where is the man in the picture from? What do you think he has on his back? Read the text quickly and check your ideas.

b ▶ CD1 T32 Read the text again and listen. Answer the questions.

1 What is special about the place where the Niowra tribe lives?

2 What do the Niowra believe?

3 What is the "Crocodile Nest" and why do the boys go there?

4 What do the boys do during the ceremony?

5 How does a boy's life change after the ceremony?

c Do you know of any ceremonies for teenagers to become adults in other countries? Are there any in your country?

② Grammar
✳ Present passive

a We form the present passive with the verb *be* + the past participle of the main verb. Look at the examples.

*The boys **are taken** to a hut*   *... bamboo **is used** ...*

b <u>Underline</u> other examples of the present passive in the text on page 44.

c Read the rule and complete it with *is important* or *isn't important*. Then complete the grammar table.

> **RULE:** Use the passive when it .... who does the action, or when we don't know who does it.

Affirmative	Negative	Question	Short answer
A boy **is taken** to a hut.	Bamboo **isn't (is not) used**.	.... bamboo **used**?	Yes, it ....
The boys .... **taken** there.	Knives .... (are not) **used**.	.... knives **used**?	No, they ....

d Complete the sentences with the present passive form of the verbs. Check with the list of irregular verbs on page 122.

1 Millions of pizzas *are eaten* (eat) in the world every year.

2 How many emails .... (write) every day?

3 Chocolate .... (sell) in almost every country in the world.

4 Rice .... (not grow) in Canada, but it .... (grow) in Mexico.

5 .... most emails .... (send) from home computers?

6 Ferrari cars .... (make) in Italy.

e Rewrite the sentences. Use the present passive.

1 People make jeans in the U.S.
   Jeans are made in the U.S. ....

2 Someone picks up the litter every morning.
   The litter ....

3 People cut down a lot of trees every year.
   A lot ....

4 Do they grow coffee in Kenya?
   Is .... ?

5 Postal workers deliver thousands of letters.
   Thousands ....

6 Do they make successful movies in Hollywood?
   Are .... ?

f Look at the pictures. Make sentences about the opening ceremony of the Olympic Games. Use the present passive.

 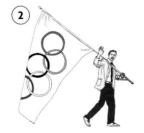 

1 torch / take / to the Olympic city

2 flag / carry / into the stadium

3 flame / light / with the torch

4 Games / open / with a speech

3 Listen and speak

a These pictures tell a story from Papua New Guinea about a man and a crocodile. Work with a partner and try to guess the correct order. Write 1–6 in the boxes.

A

B

C

D
1

E

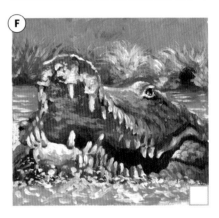
F

b ▶ CD1 T33 Listen to the story and check your answers.

4 Vocabulary

✳ Describing a person's age

a ▶ CD1 T34 Match the words with the photos. Write 1–6 in the boxes. Then listen, check and repeat.

1 a young adult   2 a child   3 a teenager   4 a baby
5 a toddler   6 a senior citizen

A
4

B

C

D

E

F

b Complete the sentences with your own ideas.

1 You're a baby until you are .... years old.

2 You're a toddler from the age of .... to ....

3 I think you're a child until you are .... years old.

4 You're a teenager from the age of .... to ....

5 I think you become an adult when you are .... years old.

6 In my country, you become a senior citizen when you are .... years old.

c How old is someone who is *middle-aged*, do you think? How old is someone who is *elderly*? How do you say *elderly* and *middle-aged* in your language?

5 Grammar

✳ let / be allowed to

a ▶ **CD1 T35** Read and listen to the dialogue. Then answer the questions.

Melissa: Hey, Andy! What's wrong?

Andy: I really want to go to the music festival in Austin next weekend – but I'm not allowed to go. My parents say I'm too young.

Melissa: I know how you feel! I had the same problem last month. My mom didn't let me go to the Cowboys game.

Andy: Actually, my parents usually let me do things. I'm allowed to stay out until midnight on the weekend.

Melissa: Really? That's cool! My mom never lets me do anything. Sometimes I think school's better than home. At least we're allowed to breathe at school!

Andy: Does your mom let you stay up late to watch TV?

Melissa: Well, yes, sometimes. But only if I've done all my homework!

1 Where does Andy want to go?
2 Why can't he go?
3 Why didn't Melissa go to the game last month?
4 What does Andy say about his parents and the weekend?
5 What does Melissa's mom sometimes let her do?

b Look at the examples.

*My mom **didn't let me go** to the game.*
*I'm **allowed to stay** out until midnight.*

Underline other examples of *let* and *be allowed to* in Exercise 5a. Then complete the rule with *let* and *be allowed to*.

RULE: Use _____ to say you do or don't have permission to do something.

Use _____ to say that someone gives or doesn't give you permission to do something.

Both *let* and *be allowed to* are followed by the infinitive: I'm not allowed **to go**. My mom didn't let me **go**.

With *let*, use *let* + person + infinitive without *to*: Does she **let you stay up** late?

c Complete the sentences with the correct form of *be allowed to*.

1 Look at the sign, Dad! You *aren't allowed to* turn right here.
2 You can take pictures in the museum, but you _____ use a flash.
3 It's OK to take our bikes into the park, Steve. We _____ ride our bikes there.
4 There's a river in our town, but we _____ swim in it.
5 My dad likes candy but he _____ eat it on his diet.
6 _____ you _____ use your cell phone at school?

d Write sentences using *let (someone) do*.

1 I don't listen to music after midnight. My parents say no. *My parents don't let me listen to music after midnight* .
2 I watch the late-night movie on Fridays. My parents say I can. _____ .
3 My brother doesn't use my computer. I say he can't. _____ .
4 We never run in the hallway at my school. The teachers say we can't. _____ .
5 We don't wear sneakers to school. The principal says we can't. _____ .
6 I drive our car sometimes. My dad says it's OK! _____ .

e What are you (not) allowed to do at your school? At home? Make a list. Then talk to other people in your class.

A: *Are you allowed to stay up late on weekends?*
B: *Yes, I am. Do your parents let …*

6 Pronunciation

▶ **CD1 T36 and T37** Pronunciation section starts on page 114.

Culture in mind

7 Read and listen

a Read the magazine page and take the quiz. Write *T* (true) or *F* (false). Then work with a partner and compare your answers.

b ▶ **CD1 T38** Read the text again and listen. Check your answers.

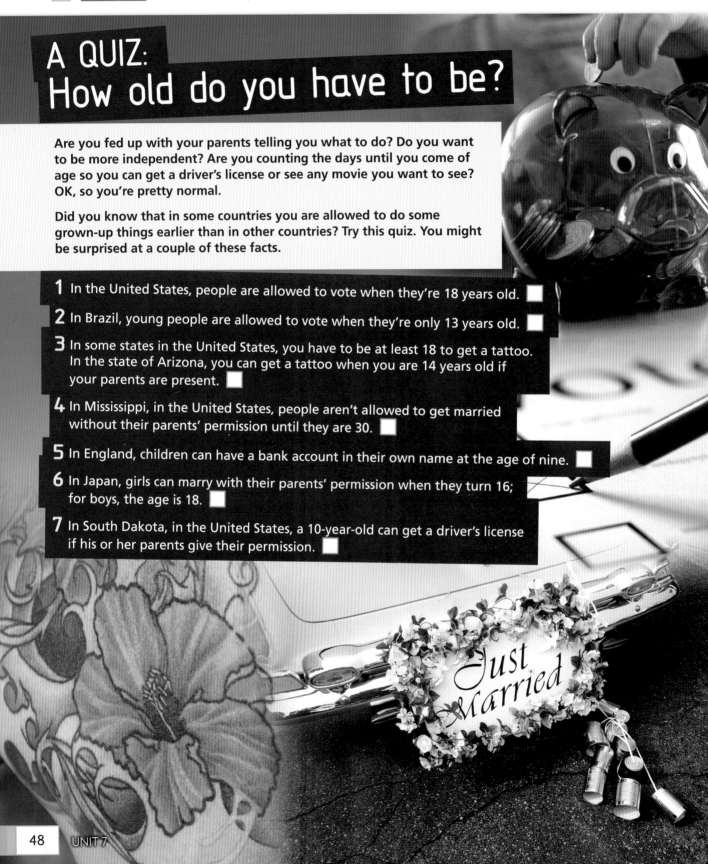

A QUIZ:
How old do you have to be?

Are you fed up with your parents telling you what to do? Do you want to be more independent? Are you counting the days until you come of age so you can get a driver's license or see any movie you want to see? OK, so you're pretty normal.

Did you know that in some countries you are allowed to do some grown-up things earlier than in other countries? Try this quiz. You might be surprised at a couple of these facts.

1 In the United States, people are allowed to vote when they're 18 years old.

2 In Brazil, young people are allowed to vote when they're only 13 years old.

3 In some states in the United States, you have to be at least 18 to get a tattoo. In the state of Arizona, you can get a tattoo when you are 14 years old if your parents are present.

4 In Mississippi, in the United States, people aren't allowed to get married without their parents' permission until they are 30.

5 In England, children can have a bank account in their own name at the age of nine.

6 In Japan, girls can marry with their parents' permission when they turn 16; for boys, the age is 18.

7 In South Dakota, in the United States, a 10-year-old can get a driver's license if his or her parents give their permission.

C Read the text on page 48 again.
Find words or phrases that mean:

1 be bored by something you have done for too long
2 not be controlled by another person
3 become an adult
4 not childish, like an adult
5 about two [of these facts]
6 not less than [21]
7 if your parents don't let you
8 become [21]

8 Speak

Work in pairs or small groups. Discuss these questions together.

1 What are the minimum age limits in your country for:
   - staying at a disco/concert past midnight?
   - getting a tattoo?
   - getting married?
   - flying a plane and driving a car?
2 What other minimum age limits are there in your country?
3 What do you think of the minimum age limits in your country?

9 Write

a Eri has written an article for her American school magazine about a Japanese ceremony. What is the ceremony for? Read her article to find the answer.

b Match the questions with the paragraphs. Write A, B and C in the boxes.

1 What is *Seijin no Hi*? ☐
2 What happens during the ceremony? ☐
3 How do the girls prepare for the ceremony? ☐

c Write a magazine article about how you celebrate a special day in your country. Use Eri's article to help you.

Seijin no Hi
Coming of Age in Japan

(A) In Japan, young people come of age when they are 20. This event is celebrated in most areas of Japan with a special ceremony, called *Seijin no Hi* or Coming of Age. On this important day in January, young people who are from the same area and were all in the same school year, go together to their local town hall, where the ceremony is held.

(B) The day often starts early for the girls, because they have to dress up for the ceremony. They wear a traditional Japanese dress (or kimono). These are extremely expensive, so most girls have to rent or borrow one. Because the dress is very difficult to put on, some girls go to a special place where other women help them. They sometimes spend up to three hours getting dressed and doing their hair and make-up. Most boys wear suits, but some wear a traditional Japanese kimono for men.

(C) When they are ready, the young people are photographed with their families. All the girls and boys then go to the local town hall or government office, where more pictures are taken. In the hall, they listen to long speeches and sometimes sing songs. They are then given a special certificate or present from the local government. The boys and girls, now men and women, then go outside, where many more pictures are taken. Finally, they leave and go out to celebrate together.

* Present perfect; *for* vs. *since*
* Vocabulary: verb and noun pairs

1 Read and listen

a Who are the people in the photos? Where do you think they are? What are they doing? Read the text and check your answers.

b ▶ **CD2 T02** Read the text again and listen. Mark the statements *T* (true) or *F* (false).

1 Playing has no effect on the brain. ☐

2 Dr. Brown has studied play for more than 40 years. ☐

3 Amy Whitcomb works for Google. ☐

4 Google allows its employees to spend time playing during the workday. ☐

5 Good students should always finish their homework first and then play. ☐

c Answer the questions.

1 Why is playtime important for children?

2 What is the meaning of the Google motto, "Work hard. Play hard"?

d Discuss in small groups.

1 Do you spend a lot of time playing? What games or playful activities do you do?

2 Do you think it's true that playing can help people be more creative and learn better? Why or why not?

3 What do you think about games in the classroom? Do they help students learn?

4 Do adults you know still spend time playing? If not, why not? If yes, what do they do?

The Power of Play

For many years, scientists have known that laughter is good for the health of our minds and bodies. Now we are learning that it's not just laughter. Having fun and playing are also good for us! Dr. Stuart Brown has studied the effects of play on children and adults since 1966. He and other researchers have found that play is good for people of all ages. Play actually leads to the growth of more nerve connections in the brain and gives us more brain power!

For Dr. Brown, play is a necessary part of childhood. As children play, they learn how to make friends and relate to others. They develop their imaginations and become more creative. Kids carry these qualities with them as they grow older.

Amy Whitcomb teaches math at an experimental school called the Rooftop School in San Francisco. For several years, she has used games to teach math. In one class, students play a game with small bags of candy to figure out what percent of the pieces in the bags is red. When they get the correct answer, they can eat the candy! Amy says, "If it's not fun, they're not going to want to be there. They're not going to want to learn."

The spirit of playfulness continues through the teenage years into adulthood. The company Google is famous for its

2 Grammar

✱ Present perfect

a Look at the example. Then answer the question and complete the rule.

*For several years, Amy **has used** games to teach math.*

Does Amy still teach math?

> **RULE:** Use the .... for things that started in the past and continue to the present (now).

b Underline other examples of the present perfect in the text.

playful work environment. Their motto is "Work hard. Play hard." Google keeps a lot of toys and games at various places in their offices and encourages people to use them. They know that people often get their best ideas when they are just "playing around" and let their imaginations go wild.

So the next time you have to solve a difficult math problem or can't think of a topic for an essay, take a short play break. Do a little dance, or play a quick game. Then come back to it. Maybe you'll be surprised at what your brain can do.

c Complete the sentences with the present perfect form of the verbs.

1 I _'ve had_ (have) my bicycle for two years and it's great!

2 My mom .... (work) in this hospital for three years.

3 .... Maria .... (live) here for a long time?

4 How long .... your parents .... (be) married?

5 I .... (not see) my friend Tom for a long time.

6 Diana and Jenny .... (be) friends since 2004.

✱ *for* vs. *since*

d Look at the examples.

*For several years, Amy **has used** games to teach math.*
*Dr. Brown **has studied** the effects of play on children and adults since 1966.*

When do we use *for* and when do we use *since*? Write the words in two lists.

~~yesterday~~   ~~a week~~   December   two years   an hour   1999
Saturday   a month   I was 11   last weekend   a long time   days

for		since	
a week	....	_yesterday_	....
....	....	....	....
....		....	

e Make as many correct sentences as you can with the words in the table.

I've studied English		I was 11 years old.
They've been married		20 years.
John has had his bicycle	for	last December.
I haven't seen Mark	since	two weeks.
We've lived here		2001.
Maria hasn't spoken to John		ages.
		yesterday.

f Rewrite these sentences. Use *for* or *since* and the correct form of the verb.

1 I really like Sara. I_'ve known_ (know) her _since_ I was ten.

2 You .... (have) a cold .... two weeks. Go to the doctor!

3 My mom's really good at French. She .... (study) it .... years.

4 I don't know where Peter is. I .... (not see) him .... this morning.

5 We .... (not be) to the movies .... a long time. Why don't we go this weekend?

3 Pronunciation

▶ **CD2 T03**   Pronunciation section starts on page 114.

Are you fun to be with?

1 You've just had an argument with your mom. Do you:

a call your friends and ask them to get together and have some fun? ☐

b lock yourself in your room on your own? ☐

c call a friend to complain about your mom, and then play loud music for an hour? ☐

2 You've just arrived at your vacation place with your parents. Do you:

a only want to lie in the sand and read or sleep? ☐

b want to have a good time and make new friends? ☐

c act miserable: you hate being on vacation and prefer to be at home with your friends? ☐

3 You've been at a friend's birthday party for two hours and it's boring. Do you:

a tell your friend you have to go home because you promised to help your dad with some work? ☐

b make fun of your friend and tell him/her that you are going to give him/her a "most boring party" medal? ☐

c start doing silly dancing or telling jokes to try to make people laugh? ☐

4 It's Saturday evening. You've studied hard for a test at school for almost a week. You call all your friends, but they have already made other plans. Do you:

a think of other people you could get together with? ☐

b get angry or depressed? You can't have fun without your friends. ☐

c spend the evening watching TV (even if you don't like the movies you're watching)? ☐

5 You've forgotten it's April 1st. A friend sends you an email to tell you that your math teacher wants to talk to you. When you call the teacher, you find out it was an April Fool's joke. Do you:

a send an email back to your friend to tell him/her that you aren't friends any more? ☐

b send an email back to your friend to tell him/her that you think it was a silly joke? ☐

c tell all your friends about the joke and laugh about it with them? ☐

6 A group of friends have invited you to come to their after-school club. When you get there, you see that none of your friends are there. You don't know anyone at the club. Do you:

a stay at the club to see if you can make some new friends? ☐

b leave the place immediately? ☐

c sit down in a corner and listen to your music player, hoping your friends will arrive soon? ☐

Score for answers: 1 a:6 b:2 c:4   2 a:4 b:6 c:2   3 a:2 b:4 c:6   4 a:6 b:2 c:4   5 a:2 b:4 c:6   6 a:6 b:2 c:4

4 Speak and read

a Work with a partner. Ask and answer the questions in the present perfect. Use *for* and *since* in your answers. How long have you …

- (know) your best friend?
- (play) football/volleyball/basketball/[another sport]?
- (have) your dog/computer/bike?

A: *How long have you known your best friend?*

B: *For five years. / Since I was nine years old.*

b Work with a partner. Ask the questions in the questionnaire and check (✓) your partner's answers. Use the Score for answers to add up the score. Then tell your partner his/her result.

12–20 points:
Your friends probably think you're quite serious and not usually great fun to be with. Life isn't so terrible you know! Sometimes it's good to have fun, and take things a little easier. And why not sometimes laugh at yourself?

22–28 points:
You're often fun to be with, but you can also be serious. Your friends know they can usually laugh with you, but when you're sad and angry you tell them.

30–36 points
You're always great fun to be with and people usually like you because they know they can laugh with you. But you don't have to be fun all the time. Maybe sometimes you should be more serious!

Vocabulary

✱ Verb and noun pairs

a Write the words from the box next to the verbs. Use the texts on pages 50 and 52 to help you.

have	_fun_	make	

~~fun~~   fun of someone   a good time
a fool of yourself   plans   friends
someone laugh/smile

b Complete the sentences. Use the correct form of the verbs in Exercise 5a.

1 When I speak English, I'm afraid I might _make_ a fool of myself because I often make mistakes.

2 Is it easy for you to _____ new friends?

3 Yesterday, Alan _____ everyone in class laugh, because he told a joke.

4 I love _____ fun with my friends on the weekend. We always _____ a good time when we go out.

5 Don't laugh at other people and _____ fun of them.

Listen

a Look at the title of the song. What does "Don't worry" mean?

b Before you listen, make sure you understand the words in the box.

landlord   rent   frown   cash   style

c Match the rhyming pairs. Then fill in the spaces in the song with words 1–5.

1 smile   a double
2 trouble   b note
3 down   c style
4 wrote   d head
5 bed   e frown

d ▶ CD2 T04   Listen to the song and check your answers to Exercise 6c.

Don't Worry, Be Happy

by Bobby McFerrin

Here's a little song I [1] _____

You might want to sing it note for note

Don't worry, be happy

In every life we have some [2] _____

When you worry you make it double

Don't worry, be happy

Don't worry, be happy now

Don't worry, be happy (repeat)

Ain't got no place to lay your head

Somebody came and took your [3] _____

Don't worry, be happy

The landlord say your rent is late

He may have to litigate

Don't worry, be happy

(Look at me, I'm happy)

Don't worry, be happy

(I give you my phone number, when you worry,

call me, I make you happy)

Don't worry, be happy

Ain't got no cash, ain't got no style

Ain't got no girl to make you [4] _____

But don't worry, be happy

'Cause when you worry, your face will frown

And that will bring everybody [5] _____

So don't worry, be happy

Don't worry, be happy now

Don't worry, be happy (repeat)

LOOK!

Ain't is an informal negative form of the verbs *be* or *have*. In the song, *Ain't got* means "I don't have..."

Very funny!

7 Read and listen

a ▶ **CD2 T05** Look at the photostory. Who is telling a joke? Who finds it funny? Who doesn't? Read and listen to find the answers.

1

2

Alex: I haven't had a break for two weeks! I even get up early in the morning to study before I go to school.

Matt: Tell me about it. I was late for school a couple of days ago. Same reason.

Kim: In other words, we're all in the same boat. We're having a hard time with school.

Emily: Oh, that reminds me of a joke. This boy comes to class and he's really, really late. The teacher gets angry and asks him, "Why are you so late?" And the boy says, "Because of the street sign."

Alex: Oh, Emily, what's the point of telling these jokes all the time? They're not funny.

Emily: Well, if you'll let me finish! Anyway, the teacher asks, "What street sign?" And the boy replies, "The sign that says, Slow – School."

3

Emily/Kim: Ha! Ha! Ha!

4

Alex: It isn't that funny!

Kim: Come on, Alex! Sometimes things aren't very funny, but they make you laugh anyway.

Emily: And know what? Laughing really helps with stress. I feel much better now.

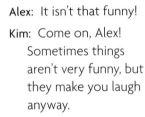

5

Matt: Well, as long as you don't make jokes about Alex and me, go ahead and laugh.

Emily: Oh, that reminds me of another one. There's this girl at school who has these really boring friends . . .

Alex: Ha! Ha! Very funny.

b Answer the questions.

1 How do they feel in pictures 1 and 2? Why?

2 What does Kim think of the joke Emily has told?

3 Why does Alex say "Very funny!" in the last line?

8 Everyday English

a Find the expressions 1–6 in the story. Who says them? How do you say them in your language?

1 Tell me about it.
2 In other words, ...
3 What's the point of ...?
4 Come on
5 Know what?
6 ... as long as ...

b Complete the dialogues with expressions 1–6 from Exercise 8a.

1 A: Sandra told me that she doesn't like you very much.
   B: _Know what?_ I don't really care!

2 A: Can I use your cell phone?
   B: Sure, _____ you don't make an international call!

3 A: I think I'm the worst student in the class!
   B: Oh, _____ , Peter! You know that isn't true!

4 A: I think I'm too tired to go out tonight.
   B: _____ , you don't want to go to the movies.
   A: That's right.

5 A: Homework! Homework! _____ having all this homework?
   B: Well, it helps you remember what you've learned.

6 A: I hardly have any money at all.
   B: _____ ! I had to ask my little brother to lend me a dollar this morning!

Discussion box

1 When things get stressful for you, do you get up early in the morning to study? What else do you do?

2 Does playing a game or laughing help you when you're stressed? Why / Why not?

3 How do you feel when someone tells jokes all the time? Why?

9 Improvisation

Work with a partner. Take two minutes to prepare a short role play. Try to use some of the expressions from Exercise 8a. Do not write the text, just agree on your ideas for a short scene. Then act it out.

Basic idea: Matt is laughing about something and finds it very funny. This time the two girls don't see any reason to laugh.

10 Step Up DVD Episode 4

This episode is about a big misunderstanding. Look at the photos. In pairs, make up a short story about what you think happens, using the words in the box below. Use as many of the words as you like. Then watch Episode 4.

studying for the exams   work non-stop
cool idea   to text about it   embarrassing
happy ending

11 Write

a Read this email from your American friend, Amy. What kind of information does she want you to give her? Why?

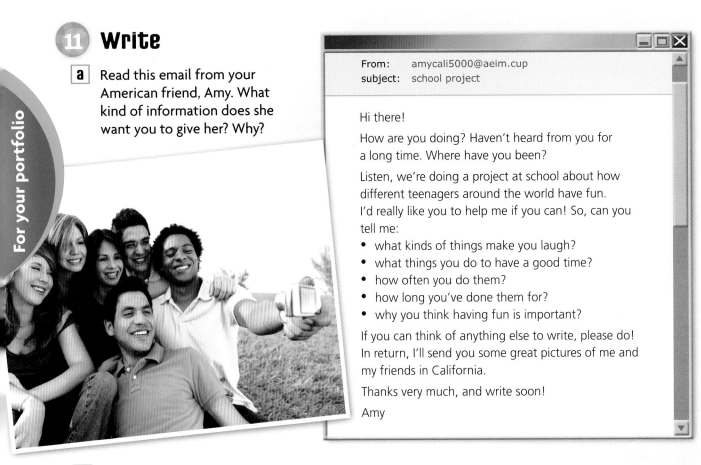

From: amycali5000@aeim.cup
subject: school project

Hi there!

How are you doing? Haven't heard from you for a long time. Where have you been?

Listen, we're doing a project at school about how different teenagers around the world have fun.
I'd really like you to help me if you can! So, can you tell me:

- what kinds of things make you laugh?
- what things you do to have a good time?
- how often you do them?
- how long you've done them for?
- why you think having fun is important?

If you can think of anything else to write, please do!
In return, I'll send you some great pictures of me and my friends in California.

Thanks very much, and write soon!

Amy

b Write your reply to Amy. Write a paragraph to answer each of her questions. Start like this:

To: amycali5000@aeim.cup
subject: re: school project

Hi, Amy!

Thanks for your email. Sorry I haven't written sooner. I've …

Anyway, you want to know how we have fun here in …

12 Last but not least: more speaking

a Work on your own. Read these questions and think about your answers.

In the last week …

- How often have you laughed? Who with? What did you laugh about?

In the last month …

- Have you had lots of good times? If so, what did you do? If not, why not?
- Have you made any new friends? Who did you make friends with? Where did you meet him or her? What do you like about your new friend?
- Have you played a game with friends or done things "just for fun"? How often do you and your friends or family do fun things together? How important is this to your relationships?

b Make notes about your answers, but don't write full sentences.

Example:

Last week: three times / laugh / in class – Sandra / very funny joke

c Get together in small groups. Tell the other students about your thoughts about fun and laughter.

For your portfolio

Check your progress

1 Grammar

a Complete the sentences. Use the present passive form of the verbs.

1 This book _isn't written_ (not write) in English.
2 Many movies _____ (produce) in Hollywood.
3 The Olympic Games _____ (not hold) every year.
4 Chocolate _____ (make) from cocoa beans.
5 Thousands of Beatles CDs _____ (sell) every year.
6 How many cans of soda _____ (buy) every day?
7 How often _____ the World Series _____ (hold)? [6]

b Complete the sentences. Use the correct form of *let* or *be allowed to*.

1 We _let_ (+) our dog go into the living room, but she _isn't allowed to_ (−) go into the bedrooms.
2 We _____ (−) eat in class.
3 My parents _____ (−) me play soccer in the backyard.
4 You _____ (+) take photographs here.
5 My brother _____ (+) me use his camera.
6 In California, when you're 16 you _____ (+) drive a car. [5]

c Complete the sentences. Use the correct form of the present perfect and *for* or *since*.

1 I _haven't eaten_ (not eat) any fast food _since_ last month.
2 My dad _____ (be) sick in bed _____ four days.
3 My cousins _____ (live) in their house _____ 20 years.
4 I _____ (not see) Jane _____ 10 o'clock.
5 I really like this CD, but I _____ (not listen) to it _____ a long time.
6 My sister's boyfriend _____ (call) her eight times _____ Friday!
7 We _____ (not eat) anything _____ breakfast. [12]

2 Vocabulary

a Read clues 1–7 and fill in the puzzle. What's the mystery word?

```
1 A D U L T
        2         N
  3       I
    4     I
  5     D
  6       Z
7         A     R
```

1 In the U.S., if you're over 18, you're an _adult_ .
2 The opposite of old.
3 A six or seven year old.
4 Someone who is about 50 is _____ − aged.
5 A more polite word for *old*.
6 A person over 65 is a senior _____ .
7 If you're 14, you're a _____ . [6]

b Complete the sentences with *make* or *have*. Use the correct forms.

1 Come on, Ken. Those jeans look awful. Don't _make_ a fool of yourself.
2 She's delightful. She always _____ me smile.
3 Let's _____ some fun tonight. We've been working all day!
4 _____ you _____ any new plans since we last met?
5 You cannot always _____ a good time. Life isn't always easy! [4]

How did you do?

Check your score.

Total score	😊	😐	😞
[33]	Very good	OK	Not very good
Grammar	23 – 19	18 – 16	15 or less
Vocabulary	10 – 8	7 – 6	5 or less

Phonetic symbols

Consonants

Phonetic symbol:	Key words:
/p/	purple, apple
/b/	bicycle, hobby
/t/	table, litter
/d/	different, ride
/k/	desk, computer
/g/	game, dog
/f/	fun, sofa, photo
/v/	vegetables, favorite
/m/	mother, some
/n/	nose, lawn, know
/ŋ/	English, long
/s/	sit, pencil
/z/	zero, those
/w/	wind, one
/l/	laundry, small
/r/	red, rare
/y/	your, usually
/h/	house, who
/θ/	three, math
/ð/	father, this
/ʃ/	shop, station
/ʒ/	television, garage
/tʃ/	chocolate, kitchen
/dʒ/	jump, damage

Vowels

Phonetic symbol:	Key words:
/æ/	bad, taxi
/ɑ/	stop, opera
/ɛ/	chess, bed
/ə/	dramatic, the
/ɪ/	dish, sit
/i/	real, screen
/ʊ/	good, full
/u/	choose, view
/ʌ/	must, done
/ɔ/	strawberry, daughter

Vowels + /r/

Phonetic symbol:	Key words:
/ər/	first, shirt
/ɑr/	car
/ɔr/	horse
/ɛr/	their
/ʊr/	tourist
/ɪr/	ear

Diphthongs

Phonetic symbol:	Key words:
/eɪ/	play, train
/aɪ/	ice, night
/ɔɪ/	employer, noisy
/aʊ/	house, download
/oʊ/	no, window

Unit 1 Word stress

a ▶ **CD1 T04** Underline the syllable you think is stressed in these words. Then listen and check.

1 bi<u>o</u>logy 2 computer 3 strawberries
4 experience 5 recycled 6 different

b ▶ **CD1 T05** Listen and repeat.

1 We recycled our old computer.

2 I studied strawberries in my biology class.

3 They've had a different experience.

Unit 2 /ɪ/ and /aɪ/

a ▶ **CD1 T09** How is the letter *i* pronounced in these words? Listen and write the words in the correct columns.

knit   crime   like   win   right   swim
risk   find

/ɪ/	/aɪ/
knit	crime

b ▶ **CD1 T09** Listen again, check and repeat.

Unit 3 *was* and *were*

a ▶ **CD1 T12** Listen to the sentences. Circle the examples of *was* and *wasn't* where it is weak. Underline the examples of *was* and *wasn't* where it is stressed.

1 He wasn't watching TV.

2 Was it raining?

3 Yes, it was.

b ▶ **CD1 T13** Listen to these sentences. Circle the examples of *were* and *weren't* where it is weak. Underline the examples of *were* and *weren't* where it is stressed.

1 What were they doing?

2 Were they listening to music?

3 No, they weren't.

c ▶ **CD1 T12 and T13** Listen again and repeat.

Unit 4 *than* and *as*

a ▶ CD1 T18 Listen and <u>underline</u> the stressed syllables.

1 Sarah's brother isn't as old as her.
2 Peter isn't as messy as his sister.
3 Traveling by train is faster than traveling by bus.
4 Jo thinks Spanish is easier than French.

b ▶ CD1 T18 How do you pronounce *than* and *as*? Listen again, check and repeat.

Unit 5 /oʊ/ *won't*

▶ CD1 T22 Listen and repeat.

1 I won't open it.   3 She won't tell me.
2 He won't answer   4 They won't come.
  the question.

Unit 6 Intonation in tag questions

Your voice goes up ↑ on the tag question if you aren't sure of the answer.

Your voice goes down ↓ on the tag question if you think you know the answer but you want to check.

a ▶ CD1 T28 Listen to the sentences. Does the voice go up or down at the end? Write *U* (up) or *D* (down).

1 You're from Canada, aren't you? ☐
2 You're from Canada, aren't you? ☐
3 You don't know much about Canada, do you? ☐
4 There are 50 states in the U.S., aren't there? ☐
5 People talk differently in Australia, don't they? ☐
6 You haven't been to New York, have you? ☐

b ▶ CD1 T28 Listen again and repeat.

Unit 7 /aʊ/ *allowed*

a ▶ CD1 T36 Listen and repeat.

1 now   2 how   3 out   4 shout   5 loud
6 allowed

b ▶ CD1 T37 <u>Underline</u> the syllables with the /aʊ/ sound. Then listen, check and repeat.

1 How are you now?
2 I'm allowed to go out.
3 We're allowed to play loud music.
4 You aren't allowed to shout.

Unit 8 *have, has* and *for*

a ▶ CD2 T03 Listen and <u>underline</u> the stressed syllables.

1 A: How long have you lived here?
  B: For three years.
2 A: How long has she worked in Boston?
  B: For a year.

b ▶ CD2 T03 How do you pronounce *have* and *has*? How do you pronounce *for*? Listen again and repeat.

Speaking exercises: Student B

 Unit 6, Page 42

Student B

a Look at the sentences below. In sentences 6–10, the correct answer is underlined. In sentences 1–5, (circle) what you think is the correct answer.

1 The capital of Canada is *Ottawa / Toronto*.

2 The biggest lake in the world is in *Canada and the U.S. / Canada*.

3 *Football / Basketball* is the most popular sport in the U.S.

4 About *5% / 10%* of people in the U.S. speak Spanish as their first language.

5 The singers Avril Lavigne and k. d. lang are *Canadian / American*.

6 Canada is the *second biggest* / *third biggest* country in the world.

7 There are *50* / *51* states in the U.S.

8 About *200 million* / *300 million* people live in the U.S.

9 Alaska is part of *Canada /the U.S.*

10 The singers Mariah Carey and Cher are *Canadian / American*.

b Now work with Student A. Check your answers for sentences 1–5. Help Student A check his/her answers for sentences 6–10.

The capital of Canada is Ottawa, isn't it?

Project 1
A pair presentation on an unusual team sport

1 Do your research

a Work with a partner. Look at the photos of unusual team sports. Which one looks like it's the most fun to play or to watch? Choose one of the sports from the pictures or use your own idea.

b Do some research to find out more about the sport you have chosen. Use books, newspapers, magazines or the Internet. If possible, talk to people who have played or watched the sport. Find the answers to questions like these:

- What is the object of the game?
- How do you win?
- What is the history of the sport?
- How do people play the sport?
- What equipment do you need to play?
- How many people are there on a team?
- What positions are there?
- Where is the sport popular?

2 Prepare the presentation

a With your partner, organize your information and make some note cards about important points. Put one point on each card. Don't write the presentation; just make the note cards to help you remember what you want to say. Find some pictures to illustrate the presentation.

> Underwater hockey – Equipment
> mask with snorkel
> ear protectors
> gloves
> hockey stick
> swim fins

b With your partner, decide what each of you will talk about. You should each do half of the presentation. Organize the cards in the right order.

c Rehearse the presentation with the note cards. Look at a card and then practice speaking directly to your audience. At the end of the presentation, give your opinion of the sport. What do you think? Is it fun to play or watch? Is it dangerous?

3 Make your presentation

Present your sport to the class or to a small group of classmates. Remember to look at the audience as you speak. Use the note cards to help you. When you finish, ask if there are any questions.

Project 2
A group presentation on green technology

1 Do your research

a Work in groups of three or four. In your group, decide what you think is the best and most useful invention in green technology. Choose an invention from the pictures, or your own idea.

solar panels

wind farms

biomass power plants

hybrid cars

self-sustaining homes

b Make a list of reasons why you think the invention is so important. Look at the example below about self-sustaining homes.

- Self-sustaining homes are buildings that are designed in a special way. They use alternative energy for heating, preparing warm water and light. They do not need any fossil fuels, light or electricity.
- They can help you save a lot of money.
- They do not pollute the environment, and they help to reduce global warming and the greenhouse effect. The more self-sustaining homes that are built, the better it is for our world.
- Self-sustaining homes are the answer to the fact that oil is becoming more and more expensive. Experts say that 100 years from now there will be no oil left, so we need to save energy and use renewable energy.
- It is much healthier to live in self-sustaining homes.
- People who live in self-sustaining homes know that they are making an important contribution to our environment.

c Do some research to find out more about the invention you have chosen. For example, when was it invented and who invented it? Use books, newspapers or the Internet to help you. Find pictures to illustrate your presentation.

2 Prepare the presentation

a In your group, put all your information together and plan your presentation. Your presentation will need to be a minimum of two minutes. Use this plan to help you.

- What is the invention?
- What is the history of the invention?
- Why is it useful?
- Why is better than similar inventions?

b Decide who is going to talk and what each person will talk about. Everyone in the group should say something.

c Rehearse your presentation. Decide how and when you are going to use the pictures you have collected. Ask your teacher to help you with difficult language or pronunciation.

d Groups take turns making their presentations.

Irregular verbs

Base form	Simple past	Past participle	Base form	Simple past	Past participle
be	was/were	been	know	knew	known
become	became	become	leave	left	left
begin	began	begun	lose	lost	lost
bite	bit	bitten	make	made	made
break	broke	broken	meet	met	met
build	built	built	put	put	put
buy	bought	bought	read	read	read
can	could	could	ride	rode	ridden
catch	caught	caught	run	ran	run
choose	chose	chosen	say	said	said
come	came	come	see	saw	seen
cut	cut	cut	sell	sold	sold
do	did	done	send	sent	sent
drive	drove	driven	sit	sat	sat
eat	ate	eaten	sleep	slept	slept
fall	fell	fallen	speak	spoke	spoken
feel	felt	felt	stand	stood	stood
find	found	found	swim	swam	swum
fly	flew	flown	take	took	taken
get	got	gotten	teach	taught	taught
give	gave	given	tell	told	told
go	went	gone	think	thought	thought
grow	grew	grown	throw	threw	thrown
have	had	had	understand	understood	understood
hear	heard	heard	wake	woke	woken
hit	hit	hit	win	won	won
hurt	hurt	hurt	write	wrote	written
keep	kept	kept			

Notes

American
English in Mind

Herbert Puchta & Jeff Stranks

Combo 2A Workbook

CAMBRIDGE
UNIVERSITY PRESS

1 My interesting life

1 Remember and check

Write *T* (true) or *F* (false). Then check with the text on page 2 of the Student's Book.

1 Brian is writing his blog at school. | F |

2 He's worried about his future. | |

3 He wants to be a doctor. | |

4 He doesn't like flying in airplanes. | |

5 He's good at math. | |

6 He can sing pretty well. | |

2 Grammar

✱ Simple present vs. present continuous

a Write the verbs in the correct form of the simple present or present continuous.

Mom: Where's Alex?

Molly: He's upstairs. He [1] _____is taking_____ (take) a shower.

Mom: A shower? But it's 7:00 in the evening. Alex always [2] _____ (take) a shower in the morning.

Molly: That's right. But tonight is different. He [3] _____ (get) ready to go out. So, he [4] _____ (wash) his hair, too.

Mom: What? He never [5] _____ (wash) his hair. Well, not on Thursdays, anyway.

Molly: Yeah, that's true.

Mom: Just a minute. I can hear a strange noise.

Molly: Yeah, that's Alex. He [6] _____ (sing) in the shower. It's because he's very happy. He asked Ellie to go to the movies with him, and she said yes. He [7] _____ (like) her a lot!

✱ *have to / don't have to*

b Write sentences. Use the correct form of *have to* or *don't have to* and the words in parentheses.

1 (we / fly to Chicago)
   We don't have to fly to Chicago.
   We can take the train.

2 (Becky / go to bed early)
   ....
   ....
   She's leaving on a trip at 6:00 a.m. tomorrow.

3 (Oscar / study French at school next year)
   ....
   ....
   He already speaks it very well.

4 (they / get good grades in biology)
   ....
   ....
   They want to go to medical school next year.

5 (I / finish the project today)
   ....
   ....
   The teacher gave us three more days.

3 Vocabulary

✱ Jobs

Complete the sentences with the words in the box.

architect ~~dentist~~ doctor flight attendant lawyer pilot

1 If you have a toothache, why don't you go to see a _____dentist_____ ?

2 The plane landed safely because the _____ knew exactly what to do.

3 When my dad wanted to sell his land, a _____ helped him.

4 This house was designed by a very famous _____ .

5 While we were flying to Quito, the _____ dropped some food on my dad's head!

6 I had a terrible cold, so the _____ gave me some medicine.

4 Grammar

✱ like, love, enjoy + -ing (hobbies and interests)

a (Circle) eight hobbies in the word search (↓ → ↑). Then use them to complete the sentences.

1 When you need some exercise, you'll enjoy _____swimming_____ in our new pool.

2 I really hate _____ computer games.

3 My dad loves _____ around the park in the morning.

4 I like _____ to music to help me relax in the evening.

5 Tom doesn't like _____ fashion magazines. They're boring.

6 Ernie and his sister love _____ to the movies.

7 I enjoyed _____ pictures of my classmates for the art fair.

8 Max and Rebecca love _____ the samba at parties.

E	P	L	A	Y	I	N	G	R	I
N	R	I	N	N	O	N	O	U	N
R	E	S	W	I	M	M	I	N	G
E	L	T	I	R	R	A	N	I	N
A	Y	E	M	B	U	T	G	N	I
D	A	N	C	I	N	G	L	G	T
I	I	I	I	G	N	R	O	S	N
N	E	N	O	T	I	N	G	I	I
G	N	G	S	A	N	T	N	N	A
P	L	A	I	N	G	O	I	N	P

✱ Simple past: regular and irregular verbs

b Complete the story with the simple past of the verbs in the box. One word is used twice.

be bring drop give have order pick up put ~~take~~

Last week Tom's dad _____took_____ the family to a new restaurant. They [1] _____ a terrible experience. They [2] _____ something called the "Exotic Surprise." First the waiter [3] _____ some chicken and fries to the table. Both the chicken and the fries [4] _____ awful. After that, he [5] _____ them some little cheese sandwiches, but he [6] _____ one of the sandwiches on the floor. Then he [7] _____ the sandwich from the floor and [8] _____ it on Tom's mother's plate! Tom's dad [9] _____ very angry. They'll never go to that restaurant again.

c Complete the sentences with *much* or *many*.

1 I don't have ___many___ friends at school.

2 Our teacher didn't give us _____ homework today.

3 How _____ bedrooms are there in your house?

4 There aren't _____ good places to go in this town for fun.

5 She works really hard, but she doesn't earn _____ money.

6 How _____ food is there in the refrigerator?

✱ *some/any*

d Look at the picture and write sentences.

1 *There are some eggs.* _____

2 _____

3 _____

4 _____

5 _____

6 _____

7 _____

8 _____

✱ Comparative and superlative adjectives

e Underline the correct words.

1 Lucy's very *tall / tallest* for her age. She's *tall / taller* than her mother.

2 That's the *smallest / most small* cat I've ever seen.

3 Do you think Dakota Fanning is a *best / better* actor than Miley Cyrus?

4 This is the *most / more* interesting book I've ever read.

5 Ruby got the *higher / highest* grade on the history test.

6 Which city is *bigger / biggest*, London or New York?

7 I love this game. It's the *better / best* one I've ever played.

8 We have a test tomorrow. There's nothing *worse / worst* than that!

5 Vocabulary

✱ Two-word verbs

Complete the sentences with *up* or *out*.

1 If you don't know what a word means, look it ___up___ in a dictionary!

2 I can't do this exercise! I'm going to give _____ !

3 Hey, Jenny. This new game is awesome! Check it _____ !

4 This math homework is difficult, but I'm sure I can figure _____ the answer.

5 I didn't like running, so I decided to take _____ swimming instead.

6 Culture in mind

Underline the correct words. Then check with the text on page 6 of the Student's Book.

1 Yarn bombers knit things like scarves and sweaters for *their friends / trees or statues*.

2 Some people say that yarn bombing is a form of *urban art / recycling*.

3 Most people agree that yarn bombing *does a lot of damage / doesn't do any real damage*.

4 Forensic science is used to *make old things new / investigate crimes*.

5 Forensic science *can be an interesting hobby / is only for professionals*.

6 Making a pencil holder from a soda can is an example of *yarn bombing / upcycling*.

7 Upcycling is a hobby for people who *ride mountain bikes / have good imaginations*.

8 The main point of the article is that *the old hobbies are the best / there are many new and interesting hobbies*.

7 Pronunciation

✳ Word stress

a ▶ **CD3 T21** Listen to these words. How many syllables are there? Which syllable is stressed? Write the words in the correct column.

> ~~architect~~ decisions decoration
> expensive graffiti information
> instrument probably

● ● ●   ● ● ●   ● ● ● ●

architect   ....

....

....

b ▶ **CD3 T22** Listen to the sentences. Then listen again and practice.

1 The architect designed a large and expensive building for the art museum.

2 In my opinion, graffiti is not a form of decoration.

3 We need information about the instruments they need for the high school band.

4 They say they'll probably make the decisions tomorrow.

8 Study help

✳ Vocabulary: Using a word web

A word web is a tool that can help you remember words that are related to each other in some way. Write a key word in a circle in the middle. Then write other words around it. For example, here's a word web with verbs that we can use to talk about *a song*.

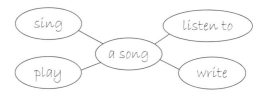

sing — a song — listen to
play — write

Practice making a word web of your own. Read Jack's description of his hobby. Complete the web with verbs he uses to talk about pictures.

I love to draw and paint pictures. Right now, art is just a hobby, but I hope that some day I will be a real artist. Sometimes I draw pictures with a pen, pencils or even with crayons. Other times I paint pictures with watercolors. I also spend a lot of time looking at pictures by famous artists. By studying their pictures, I learn things that help me with my own art.

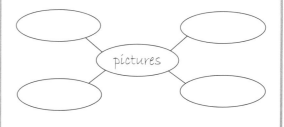

pictures

Skills in mind

LISTENING TIP

Predicting

You listen to many things in your own language every day. Think about how you listen to those things. For example, when you watch a show on TV, you usually know what the topic will be. In a class, you usually know what the lesson will be about. This means that you can make some predictions about what people will say and the words they will use. With a little practice, you can do the same thing in English.

Try to predict what you are going to hear before you listen. This will help you understand more. Ask yourself questions like these:

- What do I already know about this topic?
- What words do I know in English related to the topic?
- What questions can I ask about the topic?

Look at the directions and the questionnaire in Exercise 9. What will the podcast be about? Ask yourself the questions above about the topic.

9 Listening

a You are going to listen to a podcast called "The Truth About American Teens and Video Games." Before you listen, answer this questionnaire.

VIDEO GAME QUESTIONNAIRE

1. What percentage of American teens play video games?
   a 56% **b** 75% **c** 97%

2. Which group plays video games the most?
   a teen boys from 12 to 14 **b** older teens
   c teen girls from 12 to 14

3. Number these five game types in order of popularity for teens. (1 = most popular)
   .... Fighting games (Mortal Kombat)
   .... Music and rhythm games (Guitar Hero)
   .... Puzzle games (Tetris, Sudoku)
   .... Racing games (NASCAR)
   .... Sports games (NFL, FIFA)

4. How do most teens like to play games?
   a alone **b** with other people in the same room
   c with other people online

5. What percentage of parents think that video games are bad for their kids?
   a 13% **b** 19% **c** 62%

b ▶ **CD3 T23** Now listen to the podcast and check your answers.

10 Writing

Write an article for your school newspaper about video games and the students in your school. Include the information from the list below, and use the questionnaire to help you.

- how many students play games
- their ages and if they are boys or girls
- most popular kinds of games
- how they play, alone or with friends
- what parents think of video games

Unit check

1 Fill in the blanks

Complete the text with the words in the box.

> cans   decorate   garbage   graffiti   imagination   knitting   upcycle   urban   ~~yarn~~

Our school has a really cool art club. We meet every Wednesday after school in the art room and work on our projects. There are many different kinds of projects. One group is working with _____yarn_____ and ¹ _____ some very unusual scarves. Another group is studying ² _____ around the city. They think that it's a form of ³ _____ art. The principal is going to allow them to ⁴ _____ one of the hallways in the school with graffiti art. I'm in what they call the "⁵ _____" group. We collect old stuff that people are putting in their garbage ⁶ _____ and recycle or ⁷ _____ it into a works of art. Everyone in the group has a lot of ⁸ _____ . They have lots of great ideas.

[8]

2 Choose the correct answers

(Circle) the correct answer: a, b or c.

1 Right now Harry _____ for fingerprints on his cell phone. He wants to find out who's using it.
   a looks for   b (is looking for)   c looking for

2 Don't call Jim at 9:00 p.m. on Fridays. He always _____ *Dancing Stars* at that time.
   a is watching   b watch   c watches

3 I don't always enjoy _____ in the morning, but I do it for my health.
   a to jog   b jog   c jogging

4 A taxi driver _____ a map of the city in his head and know where everything is.
   a has to have   b have to have
   c don't have to have

5 When we _____ home, we _____ tired so we _____ right to bed.
   a get/was/went   b got/were/went
   c got/were/go

6 Ask the teacher to give you _____ for your essay.
   a some idea   b any idea   c some ideas

7 He said this was a ham and cheese sandwich, but it doesn't have _____ cheese in it.
   a many   b any   c some

8 Ugh! That is _____ coffee I've ever tasted.
   a the worst   b the bad   c the worse

9 Do you think that English is _____ language than Chinese?
   a an easier   b the easiest   c easier

[8]

3 Vocabulary

Underline the correct words.

1 Hey, we have to *figure* / *check* / *give* out that new mall. It has hundreds of stores.

2 Do you think I'm too old to *give* / *look* / *take up* the violin?

3 To become a professional *architect* / *flight attendant* / *pilot*, you have to have a lot of experience in flying planes.

4 The *doctor* / *dentist* / *lawyer* is going to check your teeth.

5 *Apples* / *Eggs* / *Onions* are my favorite fruit.

6 Would you like some ice cream for *appetizer* / *main course* / *dessert* ?

7 He *dropped* / *fell* / *picked up* his ice cream on the sidewalk.

[6]

How did you do?

Total: [22]

| 😊 | Very good 22 – 18 | 😐 | OK 17 – 15 | 😞 | Review Unit 1 again 14 or less |

2 Looking into the future

1 Remember and check

Answer the questions. Then check with the text on page 8 of the Student's Book.

1 What do Tony and Ken want to do tomorrow?

They want to play beach volleyball.

2 What does Jane think that her mother will say, yes or no?

....

3 What does Jane's mother say, yes or no?

....

4 What will Tony and Jane probably do on Saturday?

....

2 Grammar

✶ will/won't

a Look at the pictures and complete the sentences.

1 Grace thinks she *'ll* *go to the movies* on Saturday.

go to the movies

Grace

2 Harry thinks it

....

rain tomorrow

Harry

3 Sophie thinks she

....

this evening.

go swimming

Sophie

4 Jack and Charlotte probably .... this year.

go to Italy

Jack

Charlotte

✶ too + adjective

b Write sentences. Use *too* and the adjectives in parentheses.

1 Paul can't get a driver's license because he's only 14. (young)

Paul can't get a driver's license *because he's too young.*

2 Those kids can't use the playground because they're 16. (old)

....

....

3 You can't go into the theater now because the concert has already started. (late)

....

....

4 I can't wear those shoes because they're a size 6. (small)

....

....

✶ Adverbs

c Underline the correct words.

1 He's a *good / well* guitar player.

2 She plays the piano very *good / well.*

3 He's smiling. I think he's *happy / happily.*

4 Sorry, I don't understand. You're talking too *quick / quickly.*

5 Please be *quiet / quietly*! You're behaving very *bad / badly*!

6 I'm really *bad / badly* at physics and chemistry.

✱ be going to

d Look at the pictures and complete the sentences.

Evie

Mike

Alice

Cindy & Charlie

1 Evie's ____*going to watch*____ a DVD.

2 Mike _____ a book.

3 Alice _____ for a walk.

4 Cindy and Charlie _____ tennis.

✱ Future time expressions

e Complete the sentences with the time expressions in the box.

> the day after tomorrow   next month
> the week after next   ~~the next day~~
> in two years   in two hours

1 The museum was closed on Sunday, so we went back ____*the next day*____ . (on Monday)

2 It's 2012 now, and the next World Cup is _____ .
(in 2014)

3 It's May. My birthday is _____ .
(in June)

4 It's Monday. The big basketball game is _____ .
(on Wednesday)

5 It's 8 o'clock. I have to be home _____ .
(at 10 o'clock)

6 It's December 2nd. The school vacation starts _____ .
(on December 15th)

✱ First conditional

f Write sentences using *will* or *won't*.

1 We / go / scuba diving tomorrow / if / not rain
We'll go scuba diving tomorrow if it doesn't rain.

2 If / my parents / give me / money for my birthday / I / buy / a bike
_____

3 We / not win / the game / if / we / not play / well
_____

4 If / I / get / a good grade on the test / I / be / very happy
_____

5 He / not take / risks / if / he / feel / it's too dangerous
_____

✱ should/shouldn't

9 Angela wants to go scuba diving this weekend. Give her advice about how to ask her parents if she can go. Write sentences with *should* or *shouldn't* and the words in parentheses. Use your own opinions.

1 (do your chores and your homework before you ask them)
You should do your chores and your homework before you ask them.

2 (ask them when they're busy)
_____

3 (ask them when they feel relaxed)
_____

4 (be polite)
_____

5 (say that it's dangerous)
_____

6 (get angry if they say no)
_____

✳ Present perfect with *ever/never*

h Complete the conversation. Use the present perfect.

Sarah: Hi, Adrian! How's your vacation going?

Adrian: Fantastic! Chicago is the best city I __'ve ever visited__ (ever / visit). But it is windy! I ¹ _____ (never / feel) such a strong wind, especially near the lake!

Sarah: ² _____ you _____ (ever / be) to Chicago before, Adrian?

Adrian: No. In fact, I ³ _____ (never / be) to the U.S. before. Everything's awesome, but it's kind of expensive. Dad says he ⁴ _____ (never / spend) so much in three days before! And tonight we're going to a Japanese restaurant.

Sarah: Japanese? ⁵ _____ you _____ (ever / eat) Japanese food?

Adrian: Yes, lots of times. It's delicious.

Sarah: OK. Well, I ⁶ _____ (never / try) it, but I believe you! I hope you have a good time.

Adrian: Thanks! I will! Bye, Sarah.

③ Vocabulary

✳ Adjectives for feelings and opinions

a Complete the sentences with a word in the box. There are two words in the box you will not use.

> attractive ~~cool~~ dull excited exciting interested interesting ugly

1 He's bought an MP4 player. It's so _____ _cool_ _____!

2 I don't like her new dress. I think it's _____ .

3 I loved the book. It had a lot of action, so it was very _____ .

4 The tennis game was so _____ that I fell asleep after 20 minutes!

5 Jim has black hair and blue eyes. Jenny thinks he's very _____ .

6 The program was OK, but I'm not very _____ in the history of architecture.

✳ Personality adjectives

b Use words from the wordsnake to complete each sentence.

relaxedlazymeanfriendlyhonestmiserabledisorganizedpolite

1 Angela's very upset. Julia did something very _____ _mean_ _____ to her.

2 Pam's feeling pretty _____ today. Her parents won't allow her to go on the class trip this weekend.

3 Frank held the door open for an older woman. Frank's very _____ .

4 I'm not a nervous person. I'm the opposite. I'm very _____ !

5 Luke knows everyone in the neighborhood. He's very _____ .

6 I can never find anything on my desk. I'm very _____ !

7 I'm not going to do anything at all today. I'm going to be very _____ .

8 That money isn't yours. Be _____ and give it back.

4 Pronunciation

✱ /ɪ/ and /aɪ/

a ▶ **CD3 T24** Listen and write the words in the correct columns. Then listen again and repeat.

| ~~city~~ kind think time tired tonight |
| visit wind |

/ɪ/	/aɪ/
.......city.......	....
....	....
....	....
....	....

b ▶ **CD3 T25** Listen to the sentences. Then listen again and practice.

1 Can you explain why K-I-N-D is pronounced kind, but W-I-N-D is wind?

2 We're going to visit the city tonight and have a good time.

3 I think I'll be too tired to go out tonight.

4 It was very nice of you to think about us.

5 Everyday English

Complete the conversation with the expressions in the box.

| Don't panic   ~~all over~~   Just a minute |
| Let's see   you'll see   You won't believe |

A: We went ¹ ___all over___ town trying to find the perfect shoes to go with my new dress.

B: Well, did you find any? What's in the box?

A: Shoes! ² _____ how much they cost!

B: How much they cost! Oh, no! I suppose that means they were really expensive!

A: No, no. ³ _____ . I meant they were cheap.

B: Well, OK, show me. Open the box.

A: ⁴ _____ . I'm going to put them on first. Then ⁵ _____ .

B: OK, OK.

A: Ta da! What do you think?

B: Hmm. ⁶ _____ . Don't they make your feet look too big?

A: Dad!

B: Ha! Ha! I'm just joking. I think they're cool.

6 Study help

✱ Thinking in English

In order to speak English fluently, you need to think in English. If you don't, your speech will be slow and it won't sound natural. Here are some things you can do to practice thinking in English.

● Look at objects around your home and school, and think of what they are called in English. Try to make a direct connection between the object and the English word.

● When you are out in a public place, practice describing the things and people you see in your mind. For example, think, "There's a man walking down the street. He's wearing a suit. I think he's going to work." Try to think in English first, not in your first language.

● When you have to say something in English, think first and ask yourself, "What words and expressions do I know in English that I can use in this situation?" Try not to think in your first language and translate your ideas into English. If you do, you will get frustrated very quickly.

Try these tips and you'll soon find that you are thinking in English.

7 Read

a Look at the pictures and the title of the text. Can you guess what the story is about? Check (✓) your guess.

.... Helping people who get lost when traveling

.... Finding lost children

.... Helping people who lose things

b Read the text. Was your guess correct?

Lost anything lately?

Where are my keys? Where's my cell phone? I can't find my math book. Does this sound like you or someone you know? If it does, here are two ideas that can help.

First, for about $79.99, you can buy something called a "Loc8tor Lite." (Loc8tor = loc(eight)tor = locator). Here's how it works. You put special little "tags" on the things you often lose, such as keys or a cell phone. Then the "Loc8tor" sends out a signal to find them. You can have four different objects with tags connected to each Loc8tor. It will find things as far away as 120 meters.

You can also try an Internet site called "TrackItBack." This website is for things that you lose outside your home. On this site, you can register items that you often lose, such as cell phones, passports and luggage. "TrackItBack" will give you an ID label for each item. You put the ID labels on each of your items. Then you hope that if someone finds the item, they will contact "TrackItBack," and you'll get your item back.

Or you could follow the advice your parents probably give you. Have a place for everything and put everything in its place.

trackitback ®

c Read the text again and write *L* (Loc8tor) or *T* (TrackItBack) for each sentence.

....*L*.... 1 It is more expensive.

.... 2 It's free.

.... 3 It's good for things you lose inside your home or school.

.... 4 It's good for things you lose when you are outside.

.... 5 It can only work for four items.

WRITING TIP

Getting started

The hardest part of writing is often getting started. Students say, "I don't have any ideas." or "I have an idea, but I don't know how to say it." Here are some ideas:

- Talk to classmates and friends about the topic. Tell them what you want to say.
- Start writing with the first idea you have. You don't have to start at the beginning.
- Try to write for five minutes without stopping. Write down everything that comes to mind about the topic. Don't worry about spelling or grammar.
- Get up, go for a short walk and then continue writing.

These tips should help you write a "rough draft." But the work isn't done. Then go back and revise. Make sure your ideas are clear and check the spelling and grammar.

8 Write

"Lost anything lately?" gives ideas to solve an everyday problem using technology. Write an Internet article about a common problem and a solution. Use some of the suggestions above. Your article should contain:

☐ A description of the problem

☐ A description of your solution

☐ What materials or equipment you need

☐ How it works

Unit check

1 Fill in the blanks

Complete the paragraph with the words in the box.

> attractive   disorganized   hard-working   honest   kind   ~~lazy~~   mean   messy   awful

Maya's very smart, but she doesn't always do her work. She's a little _____*lazy*_____ . Frank is completely the opposite. He's very [1]_____ . But sometimes he says [2]_____ things to the others and they get angry. Luckily Louisa is a very [3]_____ person. She always has something nice to say. Her only problem is that she's [4]_____ . Her backpack is always [5]_____ , and she can never find anything. Today I drew some [6]_____ pictures for our project. I didn't like them very much. So I said to the others, "Please, tell me what you think. Give me your [7]_____ opinions." I was surprised. They all said the pictures were [8]_____ .

> 8

2 Choose the correct answers

(Circle) the correct answer: a, b or c.

1 We were going to play volleyball this afternoon, but I guess we _____ play after all. It's raining.
   a will   b (won't)   c don't will

2 For Jack's birthday, _____ make chocolate cake.
   a I don't will   b will   c I'll

3 The teacher spoke very _____ .
   a loud   b louder   c loudly

4 Doug _____ some new sunglasses this afternoon. He broke his old ones.
   a 's going to buy   b going to buy   c 's going buy

5 Today is Tuesday, so Thursday is _____ .
   a the day after   b after tomorrow
   c the day after tomorrow

6 If Alex _____ rude to the other players, the coach _____ him to leave the game.
   a will be / tells   b is / will tell
   c will be/ will tell

7 If I _____ a new dress, I _____ to the dance.
   a don't get / won't go
   b won't get / don't go   c don't get / go

8 You sing very well. You _____ be nervous.
   a shouldn't   b not should   c should

9 _____ tried bacon ice cream?
   a Have ever you   b Ever you have
   c Have you ever

10 No, I _____ . It sounds terrible!
   a never has tried it   b 've tried it never
   c 've never tried it

> 9

3 Vocabulary

Underline the correct words.

1 The Lopez family just moved into a new house. They're very *excited* / *exciting* about it.

2 The girls were *frightened* / *frightening* when they saw the big spider on the path.

3 Going scuba diving was a *frightened* / *frightening* experience for me.

4 Jake worked in a summer camp for kids last summer. It was an *interested* / *interesting* job.

5 Wow! We won by scoring a goal in the last minute. What an *excited* / *exciting* game!

6 Nan's not *interesting* / *interested* in playing tennis in video games.

7 People were *surprised* / *surprising* when they saw the statue was wearing a hat.

8 That news is *surprised* / *surprising*. I never thought May and Jim would get married.

> 7

How did you do?

Total: | 24

| ☺ Very good 24 – 20 | ☹ OK 19 – 16 | ☹ Review Unit 2 again 15 or less |

3 Great idea!

1 Remember and check

a Match the words in the columns. Then check with the text on page 16 of the Student's Book.

1	streetcar driver	ice skates	dishwasher
2	rubber	window	chewing gum
3	mice	produce toys	windshield wipers
4	after dinner	supply of potatoes	roller skates
5	summer	several broken dishes	mousetrap

b Complete the sentences with words from Exercise 1a. Check with the text on page 16 of the Student's Book.

1 A woman from Illinois invented the
    dishwasher .

2 Thomas Adams wanted to produce rubber.
    He invented _____ .

3 One summer day, an unknown Dutchman had
    the idea for _____ .

4 Mary Anderson invented _____ and
    saved the lives of many drivers.

5 James Henry Atkinson noticed mice in his house.
    He invented the _____ .

2 Grammar

✲ Past continuous

a Complete the sentences with the past continuous form of the verbs in parentheses.

1 I _was making_ (make) dinner for my family when you
    called.

2 My grandmother _____ (listen) to rock
    music on the radio when I arrived.

3 The cats _____ (sit) on top of the
    piano keyboard, so I couldn't play.

4 I _____ (draw) a picture of the teacher
    on the board when he came into the room.

5 We _____ (laugh) loudly, so we didn't
    hear the bell.

6 Mom and Dad _____ (dance) when we
    opened the door.

7 Nick _____ (try) to do his homework
    on the bus when we saw him.

b Look at pictures 1 and 2. Write sentences in the negative form of the past continuous. Use the verbs in the box.

> cook   sleep   reading   eat
> take a shower   ~~watch~~

Last night at 10:00 p.m. …

1 my Uncle James was in the living
    room, but he _wasn't watching_ TV.

2 my parents were in the kitchen,
    but they _____ .

3 my sister, Jenny, was sitting
    by the bookcase, but she
    _____ .

4 my brother, Mike, was in the
    bathroom, but he
    _____ .

5 I was in my bedroom, but I
    _____ .

6 my grandparents were in
    the dining room, but they
    _____ .

c Write questions and short answers. Use the pictures in Exercise 2b on page 14 and the words in parentheses.

1 my Uncle James / read a newspaper?
Was my Uncle James reading a newspaper?
Yes, he was.

2 Jenny / reading? (eat a sandwich)
Was Jenny reading?
No, she wasn't. She was _____ .

3 Mike / look out of the window?
_____ ?
_____ .

4 my parents / make dinner? (talk)
_____ ?
_____ .

5 I / watch TV? _____ ?
_____ .

6 my grandparents / eat dinner? (sleep)
_____ ?
_____ .

d Write the questions. Use the past continuous form of the verbs in parentheses.

1 I called you Sunday night, but there was no answer. What *were you doing*? (you / do)

2 I saw you at the sports center yesterday. What _____ ? (you / play)

3 I saw your mom and dad with a lot of suitcases. Where _____ ? (they / go)

4 You put the phone down quickly when I came in! Who _____ to? (you / talk)

5 I thought John didn't like Maria! Why _____ with her? (he / dance)

6 I saw your sister outside the movie theater last night. Who _____ for? (she / wait)

3 Vocabulary

* *get*

a Complete the sentences with the correct form of *get* and the words in the box.

confused   home   angry   ~~presents~~
wet   dry

1 It was my brother's birthday last week. He *got* a lot of *presents* .

2 Sometimes my parents _____ _____ when I don't clean my bedroom.

3 Tim didn't understand the math exercise. He _____ very _____ .

4 I went for a walk on Sunday, but it started raining, and I _____ very _____ .

5 Our plane was late, and we _____ _____ at 1:00 a.m.

6 You're very wet. Come inside the house and _____ _____ .

b **Vocabulary bank** Complete the sentences with the correct form of *get* and the words in the box.

together   a chance   ~~hungry~~   sick
a lot of pleasure   a phone call

1 When I ____ *get hungry* ____ , I eat an apple.

2 When I _____ with my friends, we often hang out at a shopping mall.

3 My sister _____ from writing her diary.

4 The last time I _____ _____ was my 10th birthday. I ate too much cake!

5 I hope one day I _____ _____ to learn how to scuba dive.

6 Last night I _____ _____ from my English teacher. She told me not to forget my homework!

4 Grammar

✱ Past continuous vs. simple past; *when* and *while*

a Complete the sentences. Use the simple past or past continuous form of the verbs in parentheses.

1   While the teacher _was writing_ (write) on the board, Toby _fell_ (fall) asleep.

2   Kelly _____ (take) a shower when her cell phone _____ (ring).

3   While Lauren _____ (watch) TV, her dog _____ (eat) her dinner.

4   Somebody _____ (steal) Dave's clothes while he _____ (swim) in the ocean.

5   Jonathan's hat _____ (fall) off while he _____ (play) baseball.

6   While Erica _____ (sunbathe) in the yard, the cat _____ (jump) on her head.

b Join the sentences in two different ways. Use *when* and *while*.

1   I fell. I was playing basketball.

   I fell while I was playing basketball.

   I was playing basketball when I fell.

2   We were listening to music. The lights went out.

   ....

   ....

   ....

3   I lost my keys. I was running on the beach.

   ....

   ....

   ....

4   Somebody stole my backpack. I was talking to my friend.

   ....

   ....

   ....

5   Danny called. You were taking the dog for a walk.

   ....

   ....

   ....

6   I was getting ready for the beach. It started to rain.

   ....

   ....

   ....

c Complete the sentences with your own ideas, or use the pictures to help you.

1   When I came into the classroom,

   When I came into the classroom, some boys

   were fighting ....

2   While I was using my computer this weekend,

   ....

   ....

3   While I was eating dinner last night,

   ....

   ....

4   While I was brushing my teeth last night,

   ....

   ....

5   While I was doing my homework last night,

   ....

   ....

6   When I left the house this morning,

   ....

   ....

5 Pronunciation

✱ *was* and *were*

▶ CD3 T26 Listen and <u>underline</u> the main stress. Then listen again and repeat.

1 A: I was <u>waiting</u> for you.
   B: <u>No</u>, you <u>weren't</u>! You were <u>leaving</u> <u>without</u> me.

2 A: You <u>weren't</u> <u>crying</u>.
   B: Yes, I <u>was</u>!

3 A: She was sleeping.
   B: No, she wasn't! She was reading.

4 A: They were singing.
   B: No, they weren't. They were dancing.

5 A: We were doing our homework.
   B: No, you weren't. You were playing games.

6 A: I wasn't writing a letter.
   B: Yes, you were!

6 Culture in mind

Complete the summary about the history of listening to music. Use the words in the box. Then check with the text on page 20 of the Student's Book.

> popular   records   ~~bought~~   recordings
> paper rolls   radio   invented
> steel needle   wax cylinders   disks

In the late 19th and early 20th centuries, many families *bought* player pianos. These pianos played music by using perforated
¹ .... , but you could also play them like a normal piano. When the
² .... (the wireless) became
³ .... , player pianos began to disappear.

The first phonographs appeared more or less around the beginning of the 20th century. The music was on ⁴ .... made of aluminum foil. When people listened to the music a few times, the foil broke. Later,
⁵ .... could hold longer
⁶ .... , and people could play them more often.

Gramophones were similar to phonographs, but they had the music on flat vinyl
⁷ .... The disks turned, and a
⁸ .... or a small diamond took the music off the record.

Sony ⁹ .... the "Walkman" in 1979. That made it possible to go for walks, travel or play sports and listen to music at the same time.

7 Study help

✱ Vocabulary: how to remember new words

a In your vocabulary notebook, record words in diagram form.

● Draw pictures next to the words. This will help you remember them.

● Add new words to your diagram when you come across them.

● Copy your diagram with your book closed. How many words can you remember?

b Write the words in the correct places in the diagram.

> vinyl records
> a wax cylinder
> a gramophone

1 ....

2 ....

3 ....

Skills in mind

8 Read

Where is the true home of the hamburger?

The kind of beef we use in hamburgers, ground beef, was possibly invented by Mongolians over 800 years ago. But who first put the beef in between pieces of bread and called it a hamburger?

Three different cities in the United States all say that they were the first to invent America's favorite food. Some people say that Fletcher Davis, from Athens, Texas, invented hamburgers. "Old Dave," as people called him, was selling ground beef sandwiches at his diner as early as the 1880s. Some years later, they say that a group of Germans called his sandwich a "hamburger" because people from the German city of Hamburg ate this kind of beef.

Other people believe that the hamburger came from a different city called Hamburg – Hamburg, New York. At the 1885 fair in this American city, the Menches brothers were selling pork sandwiches. When there was no more pork, the brothers used ground beef and gave the sandwich a new name, the "hamburger."

The third possible inventor of the hamburger was Charlie Nagreen, also known as "Hamburger Charlie," from Seymour, Wisconsin. He said that in 1885 he invented the world's first hamburgers at a fair. Seymour now celebrates the invention of the hamburger every year. In 1989, it was the home of the world's largest ever burger that weighed over 2,500 kg!

READING TIP

How to answer "true, false or no information" questions.

- Look at the pictures and title of the text.
- Read the whole text. Then read the statements carefully.
- <u>Underline</u> the parts of the text with the information.

a Read the text and mark statements 1–3 *T* (true), *F* (false) or *N* (no information). Then read the notes below and check your answers.

1 Hamburgers use a kind of beef called "ground beef." ☐

2 Mongolians invented hamburgers over 800 years ago. ☐

3 The three stories about the invention of hamburgers are all true. ☐

- "Ground beef" is another way of saying "the kind of beef we use in hamburgers." So 1 is *true*.

- The Mongolians invented ground beef over 800 years ago, not hamburgers. So 2 is *false*.

- The cities say their stories are true, but we don't know if the stories are really true, because the text does not give enough information. So for 3, *no information* is the correct answer.

b Read the rest of the text again. For statements 1–5, write *T* (true), *F* (false) or *N* (no information).

1 Fletcher Davis gave the name "hamburger" to his ground beef sandwich. ☐ *F*

2 "Old Dave" visited Hamburg in Germany. ☐

3 There is a city called Hamburg in New York. ☐

4 The Menches brothers used beef in their sandwiches because no one liked pork. ☐

5 "Hamburger Charlie" and the Menches brothers say they invented hamburgers in the same year. ☐

9 Listen

▶ **CD3 T27** Listen and check (✓) the correct picture.

1 What did Thomas Adams invent?

a ✓ b ☐ c  ☐

2 What did "Old Dave" say he also invented?

a  ☐ b ☐ c ☐

3 What did the man in England invent in 1750?

a ☐ b ☐ c ☐

4 What did the Menches brothers say they also invented?

a  ☐ b ☐ c ☐

Unit check

1 Fill in the blanks

Complete the text with the words in the box.

| get   was getting   got wet   got a terrible surprise   got to school |
| ~~got up~~   didn't get   got nervous   didn't hear   was shining |

Yesterday wasn't my best day. First I ___got up___ late because I [1] _____ the alarm clock. Maybe
I should [2] _____ two alarm clocks! When I finally [3] _____ at nine thirty, I [4] _____ . My class was
taking a French test! I [5] _____ because I only had 20 minutes to finish the test. Unfortunately,
I [6] _____ a single answer right! After school I felt better, because the sun [7] _____ ! But when
I [8] _____ close to home, it suddenly started to rain, so of course I [9] _____ !

`9`

2 Choose the correct answers

(Circle) the correct answer: a, b or c.

1 Our dog ran away while I _____ to Sarah.

   a talk b talked c (was talking)

2 We were in the yard when it _____ to rain.

   a was started b started c was starting

3 Jane _____ angry yesterday because we were late.

   a getting b gets c got

4 When I _____ about the prize, I got excited.

   a heard b were hearing c was hearing

5 The girls _____ when they saw the funny movie.

   a laughed b was laughing c were laughing

6 I saw Alice a minute ago. She _____ on her cell phone.

   a was talking b talked c were talking

7 When Lucas and Austin _____ , we were all watching TV.

   a arrived b arriving c were arriving

8 The phone _____ , so I sent her an email.

   a wasn't working b weren't working
   c didn't worked

9 When I got to the party, my friends _____ a great time.

   a was having b had c were having

`8`

3 Vocabulary

Complete the sentences with the words in the box.

| windshield wipers   invented   engine   remote control   idea   a chance   ~~dishwasher~~   surprise   got to |

1 Our new ___dishwasher___ is not as noisy as the old one.

2 Where is the _____ ? I want to change the channel on the TV.

3 It's starting to rain. Drive carefully and turn on the _____ .

4 They have a diesel _____ to produce their own electricity.

5 Josephine Cochrane hated doing the dishes, so she _____ the dishwasher.

6 Our plane was delayed, so we _____ Istanbul very late.

7 While I was listening to my favorite piece of music, I suddenly got an _____ .

8 I'll call you as soon as I get _____ .

9 My uncle lives in Australia, so when he arrived at our house, we got a real _____ !

`8`

How did you do?

Total: `25`

| | Very good
25 – 20 | | OK
19 – 16 | 😞 | Review Unit 3 again
15 or less |

4 He ran faster.

1 Remember and check

Complete the sentences with the words in the box. Then check with the information on page 22 of the Student's Book.

> shorter   ~~fastest~~   best
> slower   more than

1 In the 2008 Olympics, Usain Bolt from Jamaica was the _fastest_ man in the 200-meter sprint.

2 Brazilian sprinter Lucas Prado was only a little .... , but he won gold, too.

3 In the women's javelin throw, Jen Velazco's throw was .... than Christina Obergföll's, but they both won bronze.

4 Lucas Prado and Jeny Velazco were two of the .... athletes in the Paralympic Games.

5 At the Paralympics in Beijing, there were .... 4,000 athletes.

2 Grammar

✱ Comparative and superlative adjectives

a (Circle) the correct words.

1 She's *more younger* / (*younger*) than she looks.

2 This is *the worst* / *the most bad* day of my life!

3 Who is *the older* / *the oldest* man in the world?

4 My brother's *much neater* / *neatest* than me.

5 Is your house *more old* / *older* than mine?

6 I think Giacomo is *smarter than* / *the smartest* boy in the class.

b Complete the sentences. Use the comparative (+ *than*) or superlative form of the adjectives in the box.

> tall   happy   ~~beautiful~~   good
> expensive   successful

1 My city is _the most beautiful_ city in the world!

2 The day I married your mother was wonderful. It was .... day of my life!

3 Is the Sears Tower .... the Empire State Building?

4 That was a great vacation! It was much .... our last vacation.

5 It cost $2,500! It was .... camera in the store.

6 Bill Gates is one of .... businessmen in the world.

✱ Intensifiers with comparatives

c Write a sentence about each picture in your notebook. Use the comparative and *much*, *a lot* or *a little*.

The steak is a little more expensive than the chicken.

1 (A)  (B)

10 dollars   9 dollars

2 (A) (B)

Today: 16°C   Yesterday: 21°C

3 (A) (B)

Ferrari, 230 km/h   Fiat, 150 km/h

4 (A)   (B)

Mrs. James, 32   Mr. James, 51

3 Vocabulary

✱ Antonyms

a Complete the puzzle. Write the antonyms of the adjectives that the pictures show.

```
¹G O O D
      ²      G
        ³
 ⁴           L
   ⁵
      ⁶      H
    ⁷
      ⁸
    ⁹  E
```

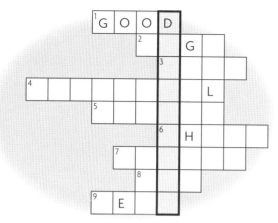

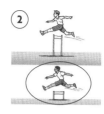

b What is the antonym of the mystery word in the middle? _____

4 Grammar

✱ (not) as ... as

a Match the sentences with the same meaning.

1 Cara isn't as tall as Riley.
2 Cara is as tall as Riley.
3 Cara isn't as short as Riley.
4 Cara isn't as old as Riley.
5 Cara is as old as Riley.
6 Cara isn't as young as Riley.

a Riley is 1.20 m, and Cara is 1.25 m.
b Riley is 15 years old, and Cara is 14 years old.
c Riley is 10 years old, and Cara is 11 years old.
d Riley is 1.65 m, and Cara is 1.58 m.
e Riley is 1.65 m, and Cara is 1.65 m.
f Riley is 15 years old, and Cara is 15 years old.

b Write sentences using (not) as ... as to describe the pictures.

Alyssa *is as happy as her sister.*
(happy)

John _____
_____ . (tall)

The TV _____
_____ . (expensive)

The cat _____
_____ . (thin)

The Australian team
_____
_____ . (good)

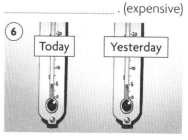

Today _____
_____ . (cold)

5 Grammar

✱ Adverbs / comparative adverbs

a Write the adverbs for these adjectives.

1 quick ...._quickly_........
2 slow ....
3 easy ....
4 happy ....

5 fast ....
6 bad ....
7 good ....
8 hard ....

b Complete the second sentence so it means the same as the first.

1 His German isn't very good.

He doesn't speak _German well._......

2 He had to be fast to catch the bus. He had to run

....

3 He's a very slow driver. He ....

....

4 His writing isn't clear. He doesn't ....

....

5 My secretary's typing is quick. My secretary

....

6 The test was very easy for me. I did ....

....

c James, David, Lucas and Jackson all go to the same school. Read the sentences and complete the table.

1 The tallest boy is also the richest.
2 David runs faster than Lucas.
3 David is the shortest.
4 James is taller than Lucas but not as tall as Jackson.
5 Jackson speaks French better than James.
6 David is richer than Lucas.
7 Lucas speaks French the best.
8 James isn't as rich as Lucas.
9 The richest boy runs more slowly than David and Lucas, but not as slowly as James.
10 The boy who has $200 speaks French better than the tallest boy.

	James	David	Lucas	Jackson
Height: 1.5 m, 1.6 m, 1.7 m, 1.8 m				1.8 m
Money in the bank: $50, $100, $200, $500				
Grade on French test: A, B, C, F				
Position in school Olympics 100m: 1st, 2nd, 3rd, 4th			2nd	

6 Pronunciation

✱ *than* and *as*

a ▶ CD3 T28 Listen and write the phrases you hear.

1 ...._as good as gold_........
2 ....

3 ....
4 ....

5 ....
6 ....

b ▶ CD3 T28 How do you say the phrases in Exercise 6a in your language? Listen again and repeat.

7 Everyday English

Complete the dialogues. Use the expressions in the box.

> guess what   that kind of thing   at the end of the day
> ~~an awful lot of~~   we're talking about   that's not the point

1 A: You want $200 for your bike? That's ¹ _an awful lot of_ money, Jake.

   B: I know it is. But ² _____ a very good bike here, Andy.

2 A: That new girl, Sarah, is really good-looking. And ³ _____? Her father's rich, too!

   B: But ⁴ _____, Paul. The important thing is that she's a nice person.

3 A: I'm going to be lazy next weekend and relax, read books, watch TV and ⁵ _____ .

   B: Good idea. ⁶ _____ , you can't work all the time, can you?

8 Vocabulary bank   Match the words with their definitions.

1 to tie   a to take one player out of a game and put in another player
2 to substitute   b the best performance in a sport that has ever been measured
3 a record   c to finish with the same number of points/goals as the other player/team
4 a championship   d to win or obtain a point, goal, etc.
5 to score   e a sports competition to decide who is the best

9 Study help

★ How to get good study habits

a There are many ways you can practice and improve your English outside the classroom. Look at the pictures and mark how often you do the activities (O = often; S = sometimes; N = never).

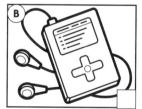
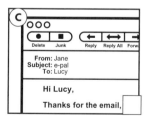

b Match the advice with the pictures. Write A–F in the boxes.

1 Eighty percent of the Internet is in English. You could try reading interesting texts in English, or find out about your favorite bands, movie stars and athletes. You could also try websites that help you improve your English. ☐

2 Get an English-speaking e-pal and exchange emails with him/her. ☐

3 Buy an English language magazine or newspaper regularly. It may not be easy at the beginning, but remember: practice makes perfect! ☐

4 Buy or borrow a book that is the right level for you. Good stories that are not too difficult are a great help, and they're fun too! ☐

5 DVDs are a fun way to practice your listening. With some DVDs, you can watch a scene in your own language first and then watch it in English. ☐

6 Listen to a song by one of your favorite English-speaking bands. Write down everything you understand. Then go online and check the lyrics on the Internet. ☐

10 Listen

▶ **CD3 T29** Brody went to the World Cup with his dad. James talks to him about it. Listen and ⟨circle⟩ the correct answers.

1 What did Brody enjoy most about the game?
   a the soccer   b ⟨the penalties at the end⟩   c the stadium
2 How long after the end of the game did they leave the stadium?
   a an hour   b 30 minutes   c two hours
3 Where did they go afterward?
   a to their hotel   b to an Italian restaurant   c to a fast-food restaurant

11 Write

Rewrite the text to make it more interesting. Use the ideas in the Writing tip.

> It was 10 p.m., and I was late for the party. I got in my car. I drove to the party. A dog ran into the road. I saw the dog. I tried to stop. I lost control of the car. I hit a tree.

WRITING TIP

Making your writing more interesting

a Read these two descriptions. Which is more interesting and why?

1 Three years ago, I went to Germany to see the World Cup Final. It was a very good experience. We were very excited. We arrived at the stadium five hours early. There were a lot of people outside the stadium. A lot of the people were dancing and singing. We went into the stadium and went to our seats.

2 Three years ago, I went to Germany to see the World Cup Final. It was a fantastic experience! We were really excited, so we arrived at the huge, modern stadium five hours early. There were thousands of happy people outside, and a lot of them were dancing and singing excitedly. We went inside and couldn't wait to get to our seats.

1 Think about the language you want to use. Is there a more interesting or dramatic way of saying what you want to say? How does the writer in text 2 say: *It was a very good experience*; *a lot of people*; *we went to our seats*?

2 Add details to your writing. One way to do this is to use adjectives and adverbs. In text 2, how does the writer describe: *the stadium*; *the people*; *the dancing and singing*? Underline the adjectives and adverbs in text 2.

3 Too many short sentences can sound boring. Link some of them together with words like *and*, *so*, *because*, *while*, *but*, etc. ⟨Circle⟩ the linking words in text 2.

4 Try not to repeat the same words too often. How does the writer in text 2 say: *a lot of the people*; *We went into the stadium*?

b Rewrite the sentences to make them more interesting. Use the ideas in the tips.

1 She walked into the room and sat down in the chair. (tip 2)

   She walked into the dark room slowly and sat down in the comfortable chair.

2 My alarm clock didn't ring. I was late for work. (tip 3)

   _____ .

3 The meal was great. (tip 1)

   _____ .

4 My favorite restaurant is an Italian restaurant. The restaurant is the best restaurant in town. (tip 4)

   _____ .

Unit check

1 Fill in the blanks

Complete the text with the antonyms of the words in parentheses.

Mom got very angry at me this morning. "Your room is so __messy__ (neat). It must be [1]_____ (easy) for you to find your way to the door!," she said. I didn't say a word. I was [2]_____ (noisy). My room is always [3]_____ (messy). Well, there are some things on the floor. But the door's [4]_____ (far) my bed, so it's really [5]_____ (difficult) for me to find my way to the door. I think a neat room is [6]_____ (interesting). When I look for my things, I always find something else. Yesterday, I was looking for my [7]_____ (old) football helmet. I couldn't find it, but I found an old photo of my sister. She looked very [8]_____ (old)!

| 8 |

2 Choose the correct answers

Circle the correct answer: a, b or c.

1 Tennis is more interesting _____ football.
   a (than) b as c when

2 I read that women are _____ drivers than men.
   a as good b the best c better

3 He plays the guitar _____.
   a well b bad c good

4 My Italian is pretty _____, but I can't speak it fluently.
   a good b well c better

5 Tom is _____ I am. We are both 15.
   a old b older than c as old as

6 Read this book. It will help you to play golf much _____.
   a good b better c well

7 This test is no problem. I can do it _____.
   a easily b easy c easiest

8 People say Chinese is the _____ language to learn.
   a difficult b more difficult c most difficult

9 I live _____ away from school than all my friends.
   a farther b the farthest c far

| 8 |

3 Vocabulary

Complete the sentences with a word or phrase from the box.

| as fast | most interesting | ~~more useful~~ | tied | zero | best | referee | messy | easy | dark |

1 For me, a new cell phone is __more useful__ than a new watch.

2 Meet Caitlin! She is my _____ friend.

3 The test was so _____ that it only took me ten minutes to finish!

4 In big cities, riding a bike can be _____ as driving a car.

5 My team lost, five to _____. I can't believe it!

6 The _____ sent one of the hockey players to the penalty box.

7 Both teams played very well, and in the end they _____ the game.

8 Suddenly it was so _____ in the cave that we were all scared.

9 For me, geography is the _____ subject. I love it!

10 I should clean up my room. It's so _____.

| 9 |

How did you do?

Total: | 25 |

| ☺ Very good 25 – 20 | ☺ OK 19 – 16 | ☹ Review Unit 4 again 15 or less |

5 Our world

1 Remember and check

Match the two parts of the sentences. Then check with the text on page 30 of the Student's Book.

1 For a long time, Paris had a big problem
2 Now the Velib program might help
3 It allows people to take a bike and
4 You can get the bikes
5 One problem with the Velib program is that
6 Temperatures will continue to rise

a reduce pollution levels in the atmosphere.
b from one of the 1,450 bike stations.
c some people might steal the bikes.
d with pollution from exhaust fumes.
e unless we do something now about pollution.
f ride it for as long as they want.

2 Grammar

✱ *will/won't*, and *might (not) / may (not)* for prediction

a Match the sentences with the pictures. Write 1–6 in the boxes.

1 Hurry up, Tristan. You'll be late!
2 Don't go up there. You might fall.
3 I don't feel well. I may not come to the party tonight.
4 I won't be long. I'm almost ready.
5 Listen, we're lost. I think we might be a little late.
6 Now just relax. This won't hurt.

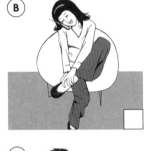

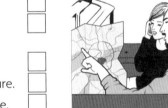

b Read the sentences. Then write *C* (certain) or *P* (possible) in the boxes.

1 People won't read books in the future. They'll only read on the Internet. `C`
2 Let's get this DVD. It may be good.
3 You'll speak English really well after a year in the United States.
4 I might see you at the party later.
5 John won't be in school tomorrow. He's sick.
6 Temperatures might not rise in the future.
7 There may not be enough food at home.

c Match the two parts of the sentences.

1 Is that the phone? John promised to call,
2 I might not have enough money
3 You won't have time to call Matt
4 I might not go to college,
5 There might be life on other planets,
6 Jeans will never
7 I may study Spanish next year

a because I forgot to go to the bank.
b before we leave. We're already late.
c but no one knows for sure.
d because I don't want to study anymore.
e go out of fashion.
f if I can find a good teacher.
g so it may be him.

d Complete the sentences. Use *'ll/won't* or *might / might not* and the verb in parentheses.

1 Maria _won't be_ (not be) at the party yet. It's too early. (certain)

2 I _____ (go) to the movies tonight. I'm not sure. (possible)

3 I _____ (not do) my homework tonight. I'm feeling very tired! (possible)

4 There _____ (be) some great music at the party. I'm the DJ! (certain)

5 It _____ (not take) as long as you think. Let's start now. (possible)

6 We _____ (have) time to have lunch before the game. (possible)

7 He _____ (not do) very well on his tests. He never does any work. (certain)

8 It _____ (be) a great concert. That band is awesome! (certain)

3 Vocabulary

✱ The environment

a Read the definitions. Then write the words next to the anagrams.

1	Wet, tropical places with lots of trees	arin frostes	_rain forests_
2	Dirty gas from cars and factories	fesum	_____
3	We find this in air or water	lotilupon	_____
4	The gases around our planet	rapseemhot	_____
5	A big building that produces energy	wrope oatsnit	_____
6	Using old glass, plastic and paper again	cringlecy	_____
7	Things you throw away	berggaa	_____
8	Pieces of paper, empty cans, etc., on the street	retilt	_____

b Match the two parts of the sentences.

1 If we want our planet to survive, we need to stop   a recycle them!

2 Electricity is very expensive, so don't   b pick it up!

3 Is that your empty candy wrapper on the ground? Please   c polluting it.

4 Don't throw away your old bottles and newspapers! Please   d drop it everywhere!

5 Have you heard about the trees on our street? They're going to   e cleaned it up.

6 People in my school don't care about litter. They just   f waste it.

7 Our river was very dirty before they   g cut them down!

c Complete the text with the words in the box.

> recycle ~~warming~~ forests garbage clean fumes pollution cutting picking litter

It's Your Planet

Why don't you care about your world? Maybe you think there is nothing you can do to stop global

¹ _warming_ . You say that you can't stop people from ² _____ down trees in the

³ _____ . You can't control all the ⁴ _____ from traffic and factories that cause

⁵ _____ in the atmosphere. But you can do little things yourself. Can you say that you never drop

⁶ _____ on the streets? You could always try ⁷ _____ up the things that other people drop,

especially in our parks. They might learn from your actions.

Just think of all the money we'll save if we don't need to pay people to ⁸ _____ up the streets.

And there's no need to put your empty soda cans in the ⁹ _____ for someone to collect every week.

Why not ¹⁰ _____ your cans, bottles, plastic and paper? Then we'll all have a cleaner planet.

4 Grammar

* First conditional

a Complete the text with the verb in parentheses. Use the simple present or the future with *will* or *won't*.

How coral reefs die

Did you know that coral in the ocean will die if people _cut down_ (cut down) more rain forests? It happens like this. If people [1] _____ (cut down) more rain forests, the world's temperature [2] _____ (rise).

If the temperature of the ocean [3] _____ (go up), too, the small animals and plants that coral lives on [4] _____ (start) to die. So, the coral [5] _____ (not get) enough food, and then it will die and turn white. If the coral [6] _____ (die), over 90,000 different kinds of fish [7] _____ (be) in danger of dying, too. So, as you can see, one natural disaster often causes another one.

b Put the words in order to make sentences or questions.

1 you / pass your exams / if / not work hard

   You won't pass your exams if you don't work hard.

2 you / buy me a present / if / I / be good

   _____ ?

3 if / I / see / James / I / give / him your message

   _____ .

4 they / arrive / late / if / it / rain

   _____ ?

5 what / you / do / if / he / not call

   _____ ?

6 if / you / not have / any money / I / give / you some

   _____ .

* if/unless

c Circle the correct words.

1 I'll give you some of my chocolate (if)/ unless you give me some ice cream.

2 *Unless / If* you read the instructions, you won't know how to play the game.

3 Will you give Marco my message *unless / if* you see him?

4 *If / Unless* the phone rings while I'm in the shower, will you answer it?

5 Your dad won't be very happy *if / unless* he finds out what you did.

6 We'll be late *unless / if* we leave right now.

d Complete the sentences with your own ideas.

1 I'll go out this weekend if

   _____

   _____ .

2 If I get hungry on the way home from school,

   _____

   _____ .

3 I'll be happy tomorrow if

   _____

   _____ .

4 If the weather is bad this weekend, _____

   _____ .

5 I won't talk to my best friend if

   _____

   _____ .

6 If I can't watch TV tonight,

   _____

   _____ .

7 I'll make my own dinner tonight if _____

   _____ .

8 If I can't do my English homework, _____

   _____ .

5 Pronunciation

✱ *won't* and *might*

▶ **CD3 T30** Listen and <u>underline</u> the sentences you hear. Then listen again and repeat.

1 They want to come. / <u>They won't come</u>.
2 They want to go to bed. / They won't go to bed.
3 I won't be here. / I want to be here.
4 So you won't play tennis? / So you want to play tennis?

5 I think you may be right. / I think you might be right.
6 You said you might teach her. / You said you're my teacher.

6 Culture in mind

Complete the summary about water with the phrases in the box.

<del>for our survival</del>   we cannot reach   needs to be moist   polar ice caps
called evaporation   have access to   use one percent

Water is very important *for our survival* on the planet. Most water is salt water. Of all the fresh water, we can only ¹_____ . The other 99 percent is in places ²_____ . Seventy percent of that water is frozen in the ³_____ . Most of the remaining 30 percent is in the ground. The soil ⁴_____ so trees and plants can grow. There are also huge underground lakes that we don't ⁵_____ . When it rains, about two-thirds of the water goes back up into the atmosphere through a process ⁶_____ .

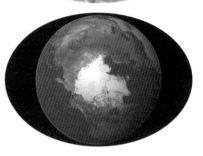

7 Study help

✱ Word formation

When you learn a new word, it is a good idea to learn the different parts of speech. English has many different ways to make verbs, nouns and adjectives.

a Look at these examples with the word *help*:

Noun: Can you give me **some help** with my homework?

Verb: Sometimes **I help** my parents cook dinner.

Adjective: Using a dictionary **is helpful** if you want to know the different forms of a word.

b A good dictionary will give you information about the different forms of a word and example sentences. Look at the example from the *Cambridge Learner's Dictionary*. What part of speech is *environment*? *noun*
What is the adjective? *environmental*

○•**environment** /ɪnˈvaɪərᵊnmənt/ *noun* **1 the environment** the air, land, and water where people, animals, and plants live *The new road may cause damage to the environment.* ➔ *See usage note at* **nature**. **2** [C] the situation that you live or work in, and how it influences how you feel *We are working in a very competitive environment.*
environmental /ɪnˌvaɪərᵊnˈmentᵊl/ *adj* relating to the environment *environmental damage* • *an environmental disaster* • **environmentally** *adv environmentally damaging chemicals*

c Complete the table.

Noun	Verb	Adjective
¹_____	²_____	polluted
energy	✗	³_____
power	✗	⁴_____
waste	⁵_____	⁶_____
⁷_____	increase	✗
⁸_____	warm (up)	⁹_____
¹⁰_____	¹¹_____	recyclable

d Use your dictionary to check your answers.

Skills in mind

8 Listen

▶ **CD3 T31** Seth is talking about school. Listen and check (✓) the things Seth likes and put an (✗) for the things he doesn't like.

1 sports facilities ☑
2 school meals ☐
3 the teachers ☐
4 the length of the classes ☐
5 the school uniform ☐
6 school rules ☐

9 Read and write

a Read the text and answer the questions.

Make Greenville High School a better place!

Do you ever complain about school to your family and friends? Maybe about the classes, or the school facilities or the food? We all have bad things to say sometimes, but we can't just complain. A better idea is to say what you think is wrong and why, and to make suggestions so that things can improve.

Enter our contest! Write an article for the school website and tell us what you think is wrong with our school. Explain the problems, and say what you think we can do about it.

This is not homework! The best article will win **100 dollars**. So start writing now!

1 What things about a school do people sometimes complain about? Give three examples.

-- .

2 What do students who enter the contest have to do?

-- .

3 What will the winner of the contest receive?

-- .

b Read Jen's reply. Do you think Jen should win? Why / Why not?

-- .

Here's what I think. Some classes are really boring. All my friends say the same. My dad says why don't we have more classes with computers and stuff? I don't know if he's right or not.

And another thing. PE classes are boring. It's all basketball, basketball, basketball! I hate basketball. Why can't we do things I like – gymnastics, or dancing or something?

Oh, and I almost forgot. At lunchtime they tell everyone to go outside. That's crazy! What's wrong with people hanging out in the student lounge? Then we could play chess and stuff, or I could do my homework (or not!).

So, what about it?

Jen

WRITING TIP

Using transitions

Jen didn't win the prize! Her ideas are good, but her style is not appropriate. Writing an article is not the same as writing an email.

a Jen rewrote her article. Put the sentences in order. Look at her first article.

☐ Second, not everyone in our school likes basketball.

☐ Finally, why can't we use the student lounge at lunchtime?

1 First of all, many people think that interactive lessons with computers could make school more interesting.

6 To sum up, I believe that these things will make our school a better place.

☐ We could have other activities in PE classes like gymnastics or dancing, for instance.

☐ Some people want to play quiet games like chess, or just do their homework, but they don't have a place to go.

b What words does Jen use to:

● start her first idea?

● start her second idea?

● start her last main idea?

● give examples of activities?

● introduce her closing sentence?
----

c Write your entry for the contest.

Unit check

1 Fill in the blanks

Complete the text with the words in the box.

| ~~pollution~~ waste reduce pollution litter pollute may not fumes atmosphere recycle will |

I live in a big city. There are a lot of cars and a lot of air ¹ ___pollution___ . Near my city, there is a big

factory, and the ² _____ are a real problem. They ³ _____ the air and the water.

Today, we have big problems with the environment, but I think life in the future ⁴ _____ be really

different. Cars ⁵ _____ use gasoline anymore. They might use solar power. More countries might

⁶ _____ levels by using clean energy, such as wind power. This will be good for the planet's

⁷ _____ . People won't drop ⁸ _____ in the streets or ⁹ _____ water. We will all

¹⁰ _____ bottles and other things.

| 9 |

2 Choose the correct answers

(Circle) the correct answer: a, b or c.

1   I think I _____ an umbrella with me.

    a take   b ('ll take)   c not take

2   I promise I _____ study all day tomorrow.

    a might   b 'll   c not

3   I don't think Krista _____ come to the meeting.

    a might not   b doesn't   c will

4   If she hears what you said, she _____ angry.

    a might   b are   c 'll be

5   If we _____ more rain forests, our planet will be in danger.

    a are cutting down   b 'll cut down   c cut down

6   Unless she helps me, I _____ her to the party.

    a might invite   b won't invite

    c don't invite

7   There'll be problems if we _____ cleaner sources of energy.

    a won't use   b don't use   c 'll use

8   What will Devin do if his friends _____ to him anymore?

    a don't talk   b talk   c will talk

9   If the weather is nice, I _____ and see you.

    a coming   b may come   c come

| 8 |

3 Vocabulary

(Circle) the correct options.

1   In some (developing countries) / polar ice caps there is very little clean water.

2   The pet food factory cuts down / pollutes a lot of our town's water.

3   People are cutting down / polluting more and more of the trees in the rain forests.

4   It took them a long time to clean up / cut down the oil from that beach.

5   They're building a new traffic jam / power station near our town.

6   We should do everything we can so we don't drop / waste water.

7   A lot of illnesses are the result of poor recycling / sanitation.

8   Recycling garbage / fumes can save a lot of resources.

9   Don't litter! Keep your environment / waste clean!

| 8 |

How did you do?

Total: | 25 |

| 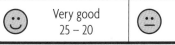 | Very good 25 – 20 |  | OK 19 – 16 | ☹ | Review Unit 5 again 15 or less |

6 Holiday or vacation?

1 Remember and check

Circle the correct answers. Then check with the text on page 36 of the Student's Book.

1 Canada is … the U.S., but only 30 million people live there.
   a as big as b (much bigger than) c not much bigger than

2 The biggest city in Canada is …
   a Toronto. b Vancouver. c Montreal.

3 … is a city in British Columbia.
   a Alberta b Toronto c Vancouver

4 The most popular sport in Canada is …
   a baseball. b ice hockey. c basketball.

5 English and Chinese are the most common languages in …
   a Montreal. b Ontario. c Vancouver.

6 It's about 1,200 kilometers from Vancouver to …
   a New York. b Los Angeles. c San Francisco.

2 Grammar

✱ Tag questions

a Complete the sentences with the tag questions in the box.

> didn't they   can she   haven't they   doesn't he
> <del>does he</del>   can't she   aren't we

1 He doesn't know the answer, _does he_ ?

2 We're really late, _____ ?

3 She can wait, _____ ?

4 They knew all the answers, _____ ?

5 Your father works in that office, _____ ?

6 Your sister can't cook, _____ ?

7 They've finished their test, _____ ?

b If the tag question is correct, write (✓). If it is incorrect, write (✗) and correct it.

1 It's a nice day, isn't it? ✓ _____

2 He lives around here, isn't it? ✗ _doesn't he_

3 They're Spanish, aren't they? ☐ _____

4 Your brother studies math, don't he? ☐ _____

5 You went to Paris last year, went you? ☐ _____

6 They won't be late, will they? ☐ _____

7 She has a boyfriend, isn't she? ☐ _____

8 They shouldn't do that, shouldn't they? ☐ _____

c Complete the dialogue with the correct tag questions.

Steve: Jane, you play the guitar, _don't you_ ?

Jane: A little, but I'm not good!

S: But you played at the school concert, ¹ _____ ?

J: Yes. Why?

S: You'll play at my party, ² _____ ?

J: Well, OK. But Mike's going to be there, ³ _____ ? And he can play really well, ⁴ _____ ?

S: I think so. But that isn't important, ⁵ _____ ?

J: Yes, it is! He's much better than me, so you should ask him to play, ⁶ _____ ?

3 Pronunciation

✱ Intonation in tag questions

a ▶ CD3 T32 Listen and write the tag questions.

1 You're American, _aren't you_ ? ☐ D

2 You're American, _aren't you_ ? ☐ U

3 She goes to your school, _____ ? ☐

4 They don't live around here, _____ ? ☐

5 I can come, _____ ? ☐

6 You'll help me, _____ ? ☐

b ▶ CD3 T32 Listen again. Does the voice go up or down at the end of each tag? Write *U* or *D*. Then listen and repeat.

4 Vocabulary

✱ British vs. North American English

a Complete the table.

British English 		North American English
1 _pavement_		_sidewalk_
2	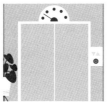	....
3		....
4		....
5		....
6		....

b Look at the pictures and complete the sentences.

1 John, can you take the _rubbish_ out, please?

2 Come on, Ann. Let's go up in the ....

3 I really like riding on the ....

4 Yea! I'm going on .... to Hawaii!

5 I need to buy some new ....

6 Hey! Don't ride your bike on the .... !

c (Vocabulary bank) Underline the North American English words. Write the words in British English.

1 I was surprised to see that my aunt didn't have any baggage. _luggage_

2 They're going to start building their new house in the fall. ....

3 Can you close the drapes, please? The sun's really bright. ....

4 There was a monkey sitting on the hood of our car. ....

5 Can you open the trunk of the car, please? I want to put the boxes in. ....

6 When we got to the bus stop, we saw a long line of people. ....

5 Grammar

★ Present perfect, *already* and *yet*

a Complete the table with the simple past and past participle forms of the irregular verbs.

Base form	Simple past	Past participle
be	*was/were*	1 ....
begin	2	3 ....
come	came	4 ....
drink	5	drunk
eat	6	eaten
go	went	7 ....
know	8	9 ....
see	saw	10 ....
write	11	12 ....

b Match the sentences with the pictures. Write numbers 1–6 in the boxes.

1 I've already eaten my dinner.
2 I haven't eaten my dinner yet.
3 They've already gone to bed.
4 They haven't gone to bed yet.
5 She's already seen the movie.
6 She hasn't seen the movie yet.

c Complete the sentences with *yet* or *already*.

1 I haven't finished my homework
   ....*yet*........... .

2 Have you heard their new CD
   ....?

3 We've .... read that magazine.

4 She hasn't finished school ....

5 My parents haven't come back
   ....

6 I know that joke. You've ....
   told it to me!

7 They haven't had dinner ....

8 Have you brushed your teeth
   ....?

d Write the sentences and questions. Use the present perfect and *already* or *yet*.

1 A: Alan, you / finish your dinner?
   Alan, have you finished your dinner yet?

   B: I / eat the hamburger, but I / not finish the vegetables.

   I have already eaten the hamburger,
   but I haven't finished the vegetables yet.

2 A: Maria / go to Brianna's house?
   ....
   ....

   B: Yes, but she / not come back.
   ....
   ....

3 A: I / buy the new Alicia Keys CD.
   ....
   ....

   B: Really? you / listen to it?
   ....
   ....

4 A: you / go to sleep?
   ....
   ....

   B: No! And you / ask me three times!
   ....
   ....

6 Grammar

✴ Present perfect with *just*

a Write *just* in the correct place in each sentence.

1 He's come home. *He's just come home.*

2 I've called Jenny. _____ .

3 We've arrived. _____ .

4 My parents have gone out. _____ .

5 The movie's finished. _____ .

b Look at the pictures. Write sentences using the present perfect with *just* and *yet*.

1 buy a magazine / read it

He's just bought a magazine,
but he hasn't read it yet.

2 buy some ice cream / finish it

_____
_____ .

3 write a letter / mail it

_____
_____ .

4 buy a new CD / listen to it

_____
_____ .

8 Study help

✴ How to remember verbs

Make flash cards that you can carry with you. Here is an example using past forms of irregular verbs.

● Get some index cards. On one side of each card, write an irregular English verb. On the other side, write the simple past and past participle forms.

| throw | threw, thrown |

● Carry the cards in your pocket or backpack. When you have time, take a card, look at the verb and try to remember the two past forms. Turn the card over and check. You can use the cards to practice on the bus, during breaks at school and at other times.

7 Everyday English

Complete the dialogue. Use the expressions in the box.

> And besides
> behind her back
> How are things going
> No wonder
> ~~What do you say~~
> Why don't

Pete: ¹ *What do you say* we watch a mystery on TV? There's one on channel 2.

Amy: Sure, I like mysteries. ² _____ there's nothing else on that I want to see.

Pete: Oh, it's starting now.

...

Pete: Why is the woman looking out the window?

Amy: I don't know, but look at the man. He's putting something in her coffee ³ _____ . She can't see him.

Pete: Yeah, they always do that in movies. You know it's going to happen.

Amy: I know. It seems they never think of any new ideas.

Pete: I agree. ⁴ _____ it's so easy to guess who committed the crime.

Amy: This is boring. ⁵ _____ we turn it off and just talk?

Pete: Good idea. By the way, I wanted to ask you a question. ⁶ _____ with your new job?

Skills in mind

LISTENING TIP

Listening and choosing pictures

Sometimes you have to listen to a recording and look at pictures. While you listen, you have to either:

- check the pictures that show things that the people talk about

or:

- choose from sets of pictures that are similar to each other.

1 Look at the pictures carefully before you listen. What do the pictures show? What are the things called in English? If there are pairs of pictures, how are they different from each other?

2 Listen the first time. Do you hear any of the words in English that you thought of in question 1?

3 If you are sure about a picture, check (✓) it. If you aren't sure, listen again.

4 Remember: You don't have to understand **everything** to choose the correct picture(s). Listen for the **key words**.

9 Listen

a ▶ **CD3 T33** Josh has been on a trip to the U.K. Listen to him talking to Megan about his trip. Check (✓) the things in the pictures he talks about.

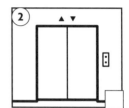

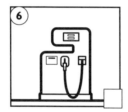

b ▶ **CD3 T33** Match the words. Then listen again and check.

British English	North American English
1 bill	a truck
2 lift	b gas
3 tap	c check
4 petrol	d elevator
5 lorry	e faucet

10 Write

a You are going on vacation to the U.S. You are going to stay with an American family in New York City and study English at a school there. Look at the list of things you need to do before you go.

A (✓) means you have already done it.
An X (✗) means you haven't done it yet.

b Write an email to your e-pal in New York. Tell him/her about your trip and about your preparations for it. Use the list and add more ideas if you want to.

Buy a plane ticket (✓)
Get a passport (✗)
Write to the family you are going to stay with (✓)
Write to the language school and reserve a place there (✓)
Get a letter from the school saying that you are going to be a student there (✗)
Buy some new clothes (✗)
Find out how to get from the airport to the American family's house (✗)
Buy a guidebook for New York City (✓)

Unit check

1 Fill in the blanks

Complete this email from an American teen to a friend in the U.K. Use the words in the box.

> apartment   have you heard   the kind of thing   take a look
> popular   subway   garbage   already   yet   ~~just~~

Dear Karen,

Guess what! I've _just_ bought a new CD by Selena Gomez. She's really ¹_____ here. ²_____ any of her music? I haven't listened to all the songs on the CD ³_____, but I think it's great. I love it!

My big news is that we're going to move soon. My mom and dad don't like our ⁴_____ anymore. They've ⁵_____ bought a house, and it's great! I'll have my own bedroom, and I can take the ⁶_____ to go to school. There's a photo of the house on my blog. ⁷_____ at it! Well, I have to go now. I have to take the ⁸_____ out. Ugh! It's ⁹_____ I really hate doing! Well, write to me soon and tell me how you are, OK?

Janice

| 9 |

2 Choose the correct answers

(Circle) the correct answer: a, b or c.

1   Lisa _____ to Tom yet.
   a spoken   b spoke   c (hasn't spoken)

2   I _____ what I'll do on my vacation.
   a decide   b haven't decided   c decided

3   I haven't washed the car _____ .
   a just   b already   c yet

4   You've read that book, _____ you?
   a have   b hadn't   c haven't

5   The capital of Germany is Berlin, _____ ?
   a isn't it   b doesn't it   c hasn't it

6   I've just seen Kate, but I _____ to her yet.
   a haven't spoken   b didn't speak   c don't speak

7   Tony and Sarah have just moved to Lima, _____ ?
   a haven't they   b didn't they   c aren't they

8   You haven't bought a new car, _____ ?
   a have you   b isn't it   c haven't you

9   He doesn't live in Vancouver, _____ ?
   a doesn't he   b isn't he   c does he

| 8 |

3 Vocabulary

Find the words in North American English for the words in the box.
(→ or ↓)

> ~~biscuits~~   rubbish   lorry
> pavement   flat   trousers
> sweets   lift   underground

V	O	T	R	U	C	K	A	C	V	E
M	C	J	G	R	W	Q	H	O	G	L
K	A	X	A	O	W	K	T	O	R	E
Y	N	W	R	U	S	K	Q	K	O	V
M	D	Q	B	B	G	L	B	I	T	A
Z	Y	H	A	D	K	A	Y	E	A	T
N	E	J	G	P	A	N	T	S	V	O
J	T	S	E	A	U	E	N	V	E	R
T	S	I	D	E	W	A	L	K	F	D
G	F	R	F	N	R	D	D	B	L	A
S	S	U	B	W	A	Y	S	Y	E	P
A	P	A	R	T	M	E	N	T	R	A

| 8 |

How did you do?

Total: | 25 |

| ☺ Very good 25 – 20 | ☺ OK 19 – 16 | ☹ Review Unit 6 again 15 or less |

7 Growing up

1 Remember and check

Match the two parts of the sentences. Then check with the text on page 44 of the Student's Book.

1 The Niowra of Papua New Guinea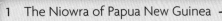
2 When it is time for boys to become men, they are
3 The "Crocodile Nest" is a frightening place, full of
4 The boys take part in a painful
5 The boys play the drums together
6 When the ceremony is over, the boys

a taken to the "Crocodile Nest."
b ceremony that lasts for six weeks.
c to take their minds off the pain.
d crocodile teeth and skulls.
e are given adult responsibilities in the village.
f believe that crocodiles created the world.

2 Grammar

✱ Present passive

a Complete the sentences with the words in the box.

is grown   are grown   's made
are made   's written
are written   is visited   are visited

1 My watch is cheap; it *'s made* of plastic.
2 A lot of coffee _____ in Brazil.
3 The Hard Rock Café _____ by thousands of tourists every day.
4 I can't read this book because it _____ in Spanish.
5 Those computers _____ in Japan.
6 Some cities in Europe _____ by millions of people every year.
7 Millions of emails _____ every day.
8 Oranges _____ in many hot countries.

b Here are some signs in English. Match the beginnings and endings of the signs.

1 English …
2 Foreign money …
3 Color film …
4 Fresh food …
5 Cameras …
6 English lessons …

a repaired here.
b developed here.
c given here.
d spoken here.
e changed here.
f served here.

c Signs like these are often written without the verb *to be*. Write the complete sentences. Put the verb *to be* in the correct form.

1 *English is spoken here.*
2 _____ .
3 _____ .
4 _____ .
5 _____ .
6 _____ .

d Rewrite the sentences using the present passive.

1 They collect 20,000 tons of garbage every year.

   20,000 tons of garbage *are collected every year.*

2 They sell a new computer every day.

   A new computer _____ .

3 They design computer programs in that company.

   Computer programs _____ .

4 People make mistakes in grammar exercises.

   Mistakes _____ .

5 They build a lot of new houses every year.

   _____ .

6 They often play baseball on Saturday.

   _____ .

3 Vocabulary

✳ Describing a person's age

a Find and (circle) the words to describe people's ages. Then write them in order from youngest to oldest. Use the pictures to help you.

teenagerchildseniorcitizen(baby)toddleradult

1 _____*baby*_____   4 _____

2 _____   5 _____

3 _____   6 _____

b Complete the sentences. Use words from Exercise 3a.

1 In many countries, you become an __*adult*__ when you're 18 years old.

2 My older sister had a _____ last month. His name's Lucas.

3 My little brother's only eight. He's still a _____ .

4 It's great to be a _____ ! I can do a lot of things I couldn't do when I was a child.

5 My grandmother's 68, so she's a _____ citizen.

6 My cousin Jackson's only 18 months old, so he's a _____ .

c **Vocabulary bank** Complete the sentences with the words in the box.

~~come of age~~ getting on adulthood look her age act your age youth

1 In many cultures, when teenagers _*come of age*_ , they go through a special ceremony.

2 Come on, Sue, _____ _____ ! You're not a child any more.

3 My parents are still very active, but they are _____ in years now.

4 My dad always says that school rules were much stricter in his _____ than they are now.

5 _____ is a time when there are a lot of responsibilities waiting for you.

6 Your mom looks like your sister! She doesn't _____ at all.

4 Grammar

★ let / be allowed to

a Write the negatives of the underlined verbs.

1 We<u>'re allowed to</u> stay out late.
   We're not allowed to stay out late.

2 I<u>'m allowed to</u> watch TV until 11:30.
   ....

3 You<u>'re allowed to</u> bike here.
   ....

4 The teacher <u>lets</u> us leave early.
   ....

5 Our parents <u>let</u> us play football in the yard.
   ....

6 My brother <u>lets</u> me use his computer.
   ....

b Look at the pictures and complete the sentences with the correct form of *be allowed to*.

Oh, no! We *'re not allowed to* take pictures here.

Sorry, sir. You .... park here.

OK, let's go, Jacob. We .... bike here.

Oh, no! We .... play soccer here.

I ....
wear jeans at my school.

Sophia, remember that you .... eat or drink inside the library.

c Look at the pictures. Write sentences using *(not) let (someone) do* or *(not) be allowed to*.

1 Our father / play soccer in the yard
   Our father doesn't let us play soccer in the yard.

2 We / wear jeans to school
   ....
   ....

3 We / run in the school hallways
   ....
   ....

4 My sister / our cat / sleep on her bed
   ....
   ....

5 My parents / me / put posters on my wall
   ....
   ....
   ....

6 Teenagers / go into that dance club
   ....
   ....
   ....

5 Pronunciation

✱ /oʊ/ and /aʊ/

a ▶ **CD3 T34** Write the words from the box in the correct columns. Then listen and check.

> ~~know~~ ~~now~~ show sound low loud around throw shout town house go down allowed

/oʊ/	/aʊ/	
know	*now*	

b ▶ **CD3 T35** Say these sentences. Then listen, check and repeat.

1 Let's go downtown.
2 We aren't allowed to go out.
3 Don't shout so loudly!
4 The kids are running around the house.
5 Can you pronounce this sound?

6 Culture in mind

7 Study help

✱ Pronunciation: using a dictionary

a A dictionary can help you pronounce new words, if it provides phonetic symbols. Check the Phonetic symbols list on page 114 of the Student's Book. The letter(s) in bold in the word next to the symbol shows you how to say the sound of each symbol.

b Here are four words from Unit 7. Check their pronunciation in a dictionary. Look at the symbols for the underlined vowels.

al**l**ow   tr**i**be
cerem**o**ny   bamb**oo**

c Now look up these words in a dictionary. Write their pronunciation using phonetic symbols.

mouse ....

though ....

straight ....

comb ....

Circle the correct option in each sentence. Then check with the quiz on page 48 of your Student's Book.

1 In Brazil, you *have /* (*are allowed*) to vote when you are 16.
2 In the state of Arizona, the parents *have / are allowed* to be present when a 14-year-old gets a tattoo.
3 In England, children can *have / must have* a bank account at the age of seven.
4 In Mississippi, people *can / aren't allowed to* get married until age 30 without their parents' permission.
5 In Japan, girls *are / aren't* allowed to get married before they are 16.
6 In the state of South Dakota, 12-year-olds *are / aren't* allowed to drive a car.

Skills in mind

8 Read

a Read this email from Mike to his friend Amy. Why is he writing to Amy?

_____

_____

_____

> ● ● ●
>
> Hi, Amy!
>
> How are things? Hope you're OK. Sorry I haven't replied to your last email, but I've just finished my school science project.
>
> Listen, it's my 16th birthday on June 17, and I'm having a party at my place. Can you come? Hope you can. The party will be great, and all my friends are going to be there. Let me know, OK?
>
> See you!
>
> Mike

b Read Amy's reply. Can she go to Mike's party?

> ● ● ●
>
> Hi, Mike!
>
> How are you? Hope you're OK and your project went well.
>
> Thanks a lot for your email. It was good to hear from you. Thanks, too, for the invitation to your birthday party on the 17th, but we're going on vacation on the 10th and we aren't coming back until the 20th. I'm sorry, but there's no way I can go. But I hope you have a really good time and enjoy the party.
>
> I'm really excited about our vacation because we're going to the Bahamas! Can't wait – it's my first time! A lot of sun and swimming, I hope. It'll be great! You won't get a postcard from me, of course. You know I'm too lazy! Well, I have loads of other emails to write, so I'll end here.
>
> Take care and write again soon.
>
> Love,
>
> Amy

c Read the email again and write _T_ (true) or _F_ (false).

1 Amy and her family are going on vacation on June 17. [F]

2 Amy's family will be on vacation for two weeks. [ ]

3 Amy has never been to the Bahamas before. [ ]

4 She wants to do a lot of swimming on vacation. [ ]

5 Mike will get a postcard from Amy. [ ]

6 Amy has to write a lot of other emails. [ ]

WRITING TIP

Informal letters and emails

When you write emails or letters to friends, use an informal style. Study these examples:

- Begin the email/letter with _Hi_ (name), or _Hey_ (name). (You can also use _Dear_ (name) for informal or more formal emails/letters.)

- At the end, write _Love, See you, Write soon_ or _Take care_ before you write your name.

- In the email/letter, use contractions or short forms. For example: _I'm_ (not _I am_), _we're_ (not _we are_), _he doesn't_ (not _he does not_), etc.

- Show interest in the person you're writing to. Use expressions like: _How are things with you?, Is everything OK?, I hope you're OK, Thanks for your (last) email/letter_, etc.

- In very informal writing, sometimes _I_ or _you_ are left out, when it is clear who the subject is. For example, _Hope you're OK_, instead of _I hope you're well._

Underline examples of informal style in the emails in Exercises 8a and 8b.

9 Write

Imagine you get an email from your American e-pal, inviting you to go and stay with him/her next summer. You can't go because you have planned to spend your summer somewhere else. Write an email to reply to your e-pal. Use Amy's email to help you.

Unit check

1 Fill in the spaces

Complete the text with the words in the box.

> child   baby   get married   let   given   ~~age~~   adult   toddler   senior citizen   allowed to

What's the best _age_ in life? When you are a [1] _____ , life is simple. You're happy if you are
[2] _____ enough food and milk and your parents look after you. Then, as a [3] _____ , you learn
to walk and begin to discover the world around you. When I was a [4] _____ , my life was great. I loved
it when I started school and learned to read and write. But I wasn't happy when my parents didn't
[5] _____ me stay up late or watch TV. Perhaps being an [6] _____ is the best time in life. You're
[7] _____ drive a car and vote, and you can [8] _____ , if you find the right person, of course!
Or is it best to be a [9] _____ , like my grandfather? He's 72, and he's always happy!

| 9 |

2 Choose the correct answers

Circle the correct answer: a, b or c.

1 How many cars _____ every day in the U.S.?

   a (are produced)   b produce   c produced

2 Too much energy _____ all over the world.

   a is wasted   b was wasted   c wasting

3 You _____ to sit here.

   a aren't allowed   b isn't allowed   c don't allow

4 His parents _____ go out on weekdays.

   a let him to   b let him   c are let him

5 _____ your brother let you borrow his sneakers?

   a Is   b Does   c Do

6 Some Australian animals _____ in any other country.

   a are not found   b is not found   c don't find

7 These days, cars _____ with the help of computers.

   a is designed   b am designed   c are designed

8 A lot of ice cream _____ every summer.

   a is eaten   b were eaten   c are eaten

9 Susan's parents _____ go to dance clubs.

   a doesn't let her   b don't let her   c allowed to

| 8 |

3 Vocabulary

Complete the sentences with the words in the box.

> underage   at least   grounded   youth
> childhood   come of age   ~~baby~~
> until   act your age

1 My little brother is still a _baby_ . He can't walk yet.

2 My friends and I are all counting the days until we _____ .

3 She's not a very happy person because she had a difficult _____ .

4 I think in most countries you have to be _____ 18 to drive a car.

5 Stop playing silly games! You're 17, so _____ .

6 Dad says he played football in his _____ .

7 I can't watch that movie because I'm only 12. I'm _____ .

8 Lisa is really tired of being _____ when she stays out late.

9 In some places, you're not allowed to drive a car _____ you are 16.

| 8 |

How did you do?

Total: | 25 |

|  | Very good 25 – 20 | | OK 19 – 16 | 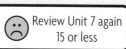 | Review Unit 7 again 15 or less |

8 Have fun!

1 Remember and check

Fill in the blanks with the correct words. Then check with the text on page 50 of the Student's Book.

1 Laughter is good for the ___health___ of our minds and bodies.

2 Dr. Stuart Brown has discovered that play leads to the growth of more nerve connections in the _____ .

3 As children play, they develop their imaginations and become more _____ .

4 Amy Whitcomb is a teacher who uses _____ to teach math.

5 Some companies like Google believe that a _____ workplace helps their employees get better ideas.

6 When students are having problems with their _____ , they should take a short play break.

2 Grammar

✻ Present perfect

a Check (✓) the correct sentence in each pair. Put an X (✗) next to the incorrect sentence.

1 a Jon lives here since 1999. ✗
  b Jon has lived here since 1999. ✓

2 a I've had my bike for two years. ☐
  b I have my bike for two years. ☐

3 a A: How long are you here? ☐
    B: Since eight o'clock.
  b A: How long have you been here? ☐
    B: Since eight o'clock.

4 a I haven't been to school since last week. ☐
  b I haven't been to school for last week. ☐

5 a My mom has worked here for three months. ☐
  b My mom has worked here since three months. ☐

6 a I've seen that movie three times. ☐
  b I see that movie three times. ☐

b Clown Doctors are clowns who help children in hospitals by playing with them and making them laugh. Complete the text about a Clown Doctor. Use the present perfect of the verbs in parentheses.

Dr. Helen Marsden talks about Fran Mason, a Clown Doctor.

The Clown Doctor, Fran Mason, _has visited_ (visit) us every month since 2002. Little James Wallace is only five years old, but he [1] _____ (be) in the hospital for four months. He has a lot of fun when the Clown Doctor's here. James [2] _____ (have) three operations since last month, but he's getting much better. James's parents [3] _____ (tell) us the Clown Doctor's visits [4] _____ (help) him to get better. Since Fran's last visit, James [5] _____ (ask) many times when she's coming back. We [6] _____ (arrange) for Fran to come back next week, so James is very happy!

c Complete the questions. Use *How long* and the present perfect of the verbs in parentheses.

1 A: Maria and Marco live in Rome.
  B: _How long have they lived_ (live) there?

2 A: I have a new bike!
  B: Really? _____ (have) it?

3 A: My sister's in Paris.
  B: _____ (be) there?

4 A: My older brother works in that factory.
  B: _____ (work) there?

5 A: My dad studies Chinese at night school.
  B: _____ (study) Chinese?

d Complete the text. Use the simple present or the present perfect of the verbs in parentheses.

Hakan Tasan is 21 and he's from Turkey, but he _lives_ (live) in Dallas, Texas. He ¹ _____ (live) there for almost two years, and he ² _____ (love) it. He ³ _____ (be) a soccer player with a Dallas team. He ⁴ _____ (play) goalie, but he ⁵ _____ (not play) any games for three months because of an injured foot. "I ⁶ _____ (want) to play again very soon," Hakan says. "Since January, my foot ⁷ _____ (get) much better, so I ⁸ _____ (hope) that next month I'll be back on the team."

3 Grammar

* *for* vs. *since*

a Complete the sentences with *for* and *since*.

1 We've lived in this house ___for___ a long time.
  ___since___ 1998.

2 My uncle's been here _____ Saturday.
  _____ two days.

3 I haven't eaten anything _____ yesterday.
  _____ 24 hours.

4 Our team hasn't won _____ six months!
  _____ last July!

5 Andy hasn't called me _____ last weekend.
  _____ a week.

6 I've studied at this school _____ a very long time!
  _____ I was 11.

b Look at the pictures and write sentences. Use the present perfect and *for* or *since*.

1 Tom / be in the library

Tom's been in the library since nine o'clock.

Tom's been in the library for two hours.

2006   now

2 They / live in this house

_____ .

_____ .

Sunday   Tuesday

3 I / be sick

_____ .

_____ .

2008   now

4 My aunt / have her car

_____ .

_____ .

2007   now

5 We / have this computer

_____ .

_____ .

C Complete the sentences. Use the present perfect form of the verbs in parentheses and *for* or *since*.

1 Paula's hungry. She
  hasn't eaten (not
  eat) _since_ breakfast
  this morning.

2 Tom's hair is too long.
  He _____
  (not cut) it _____
  three years.

3 It's terrible!
  My girlfriend
  _____
  (not call) me _____
  Saturday!

4 I'm bored!
  I _____ (not be)
  out _____
  yesterday.

5 Mike and John
  aren't happy. They
  _____
  (not play) soccer
  _____ two weeks.

6 I hope the
  movie's good. I
  _____
  (not see) a good movie
  _____ a long time.

d Write six true sentences about you / your family / your friends. Use the present perfect and *for* or *since*.

I've lived in this town since I was three years old.   *Carlo and I have been friends for three years.*

1 I / live / this town _____ .

2 I / have / (my computer / my bicycle / my dog / my cat) _____ .

3 I / be / friends with _____ .

4 _____ .

5 _____ .

6 _____ .

4 Pronunciation

✻ *have, has* and *for*

a ▶ CD3 T36 Read the sentences and <u>underline</u> the words you think are stressed. Then listen, check and repeat. Pay special attention to the pronunciation of *has* and *have*.

1 <u>Where</u> have you <u>been</u>?
2 How long has he been there?
3 My parents have bought a new car.
4 James has gone home.

b ▶ CD3 T37 Now read these sentences. <u>Underline</u> the words you think are stressed. Then listen, check and repeat. Pay special attention to the pronunciation of *for*.

1 He's <u>been</u> here for <u>many years</u>.
2 We've lived here for a long time.
3 I've had this bike for three months.
4 We haven't eaten for two hours.

5 Vocabulary

✱ Verb and noun pairs

a Complete the sentences. Use the correct form of *have* or *make*.

1 Last night's party was great! We really
   had fun.

2 It's my birthday next Saturday, so don't
   .... any plans.

3 I didn't do very well. I .... four
   mistakes!

4 I fell off my bike and my friends ....
   fun of me.

5 The class trip was great. We .... a
   good time.

6 The Clown Doctor was .... funny
   faces!

b **Vocabulary bank** Complete the text. Use
the correct form of *have*, *make* or *take*.

Dear Annie,

I [1] .... a problem. Next Friday, I have
to [2] .... my driving test. I'm really
nervous because last week I [3] ....
an accident during my driving lesson. Until
then, I [4] .... a lot of progress, but
now I think I should [5] .... a break and
cancel the test. What should I do? I have to
[6] .... a decision today!

Thanks, Emma

6 Everyday English

Complete the dialogue. Use the
expressions in the box.

> in other words   What's the point of
> come on   as long as
> ~~Tell me about it~~   Know what

Sharon: Hi, Ben. It's me, Sharon. Have you
finished your homework?

Ben: Yes. It was really hard, though!

Sharon: _Tell me about it_ ! I worked from six
o'clock until now! So, what are you doing?

Ben: Me? I'm playing my new computer game.

Sharon: Oh, Ben! [1] .... playing
computer games? They're a waste of time.

Ben: No, they aren't. You can learn a lot from
a computer game, [2] .... you
choose the right one.

Sharon: Oh, [3] .... ! You aren't
playing the game because it's educational!

Ben: No, you're right. I'm playing it because it's
fun. That's the most important thing right now.

Sharon: Ah! So, [4] .... , it's a game
first and a learning thing second. See? I'm
right. It's a waste of time!

Ben: Oh, Sharon. [5] .... ? I need to
relax. So I'm going back to my game. Thanks
for calling. Bye!

7 Study help

✱ How to learn English tenses

a You may find some English tenses like the
present perfect difficult. Read these ideas to
help you.

- Underline examples of the present perfect in the
  Student's Book and the Workbook. Do the same
  with any songs in English that you know.

- When you read, find examples of the present
  perfect. Think about **why** it is used.

- When you listen to your teacher (or other English
  speakers), listen for examples of the present
  perfect and think about why he/she has used it.

- Learn from your mistakes! It's OK to make
  mistakes and it's a normal part of learning.

b Read the paragraph below. Underline examples
of the present perfect.

LA student wins trip to Buenos Aires

Mike Bennet, a student from Los Angeles, California,
has won first prize in a competition for student
computer programmers. Michael is 19 and studied at
Berkeley High School in Berkeley, California, before
going to the University of California in Los Angeles
(UCLA). He has been interested in computing since he
was 12, and he has already written several pieces of
software. Michael has only studied programming at
UCLA for one year. He entered the competition when
a professor suggested that he could do well.

Skills in mind

How to answer multiple choice questions

- Read the whole text first, before you look at the questions and options. Use the title and picture(s) to help you understand the whole text. Look at the title and picture of the text on this page. What do you think the text is about?

- Read each question and the options carefully. <u>Underline</u> the most important (key) words in each question. Look at **question 1**. The key words are *Hunter Adams*, *went*, *Virginia*, *because*. Find the part of the text that has the answer. Words like *Virginia* are easy to find because they start with a capital letter.

- Read that part of the text carefully again.

- Usually there is at least one option that is clearly wrong because it states something that is completely different from the information in the text. In **question 1**, *a* is wrong because at the start of the second paragraph it says that Adams went to Virginia *after* he left the hospital.

- Remember: you don't have to understand **everything** in the text. The exercise asks you to find the answers to the questions, not to understand all the words in the text.

8 Read

Read the text and ⟨circle⟩ the correct answer: a, b or c.

Hunter "Patch" Adams

When he was a teenager, Hunter Adams was very unhappy, and he spent many years in the 1960s and 1970s in a hospital for people with mental health problems.

When he left the hospital, Adams decided to become a doctor, so he went to medical school in the state of Virginia, in the U.S. There he often did things differently from the doctors and other students. For example, he didn't like the doctors' white coats, so he wore shirts with flowers on them when he visited his patients. He also tried to make them laugh. The doctors at the medical school didn't like Adams because he was too different.

But Adams believed that people in a hospital need more than medicine. He saw that patients were lonely and unhappy. He tried to help them, not just as patients but as people, too. He spent a lot of time with children in the hospital. He often put on a red nose to look like a clown and to make the children laugh.

When he finished medical school and became a doctor, Adams and some other doctors began an organization called the Gesundheit Institute. One of their goals is to build a clinic and teaching center. It will be a place with a different way of working with sick people.

Hunter Adams became famous during the 1980s, and in 1998, Universal Pictures made a successful movie about Adams's life called *Patch Adams*. Robin Williams played Adams. Williams said, "Hunter is a really warm person, who believes that patients need a doctor who's a friend. I enjoyed playing him."

1 Hunter Adams went to Virginia because …
   a he had mental health problems.
   (b) he wanted to be a doctor.
   c he did things differently.

2 Adams wore shirts with flowers on them because …
   a he didn't want to wear a white coat.
   b the doctors didn't like him.
   c it made the patients laugh.

3 Adams thought that many people the in hospital …
   a didn't need medicine.
   b were unhappy and lonely.
   c weren't nice people.

4 Adams started the Gesundheit Institute …
   a with other doctors.
   b on his own.
   c with different sick people.

5 Universal Pictures made a movie about Hunter Adams because …
   a Adams built a successful hospital.
   b Robin Williams was Adams's friend.
   c Adams was a famous person.

Unit check

1 Fill in the blanks

Complete the text with the words in the box.

| funny faces   makes fun   since   made fools   ~~to laugh~~   time   for   make me   haven't   fun |

I love __to laugh__ , and I like people who [1] _____ laugh, like my best friend, Sarah. I've known her [2] _____ nine years, and she's really great. She loves telling jokes, but she never [3] _____ of other people. On weekends, we usually have a lot of [4] _____ . We often go to the park and have a soda and a good [5] _____ together. But one Sunday, a few weeks ago, we [6] _____ of ourselves! We were sitting under a tree in the park, making [7] _____ for about half an hour. Then we saw that two boys from my class were watching us! We [8] _____ been to the park [9] _____ that Sunday! | 9 |

2 Choose the correct answers

Circle the correct answer: a, b or c.

1   Jacob is nice. He _____ in my class since December.
    a (has been)   b is   c was

2   How long _____ this bike?
    a you had   b have you   c have you had

3   I'm going to see my cousin next week. We _____ each other for two years.
    a don't see   b haven't seen   c didn't see

4   My parents _____ for 15 years.
    a have been married   b have married   c are married

5   David _____ with us since last summer.
    a has been   b is   c was

6   I'm sorry I _____ since we last spoke. I've been so busy!
    a didn't call   b haven't called   c don't call

7   You must be hungry. You _____ since last night.
    a haven't eaten   b didn't eat   c hasn't eaten

8   My sister has hated tomato soup _____ she was a child.
    a for   b when   c since

9   Carol and I _____ e-pals for three years.
    a have been   b are   c been | 8 |

3 Vocabulary

Complete the sentences. Use the correct form of *make* or *take*.

1   When you called we _were making_ dinner.

2   I think we need to _____ a plan before we start.

3   We aren't in a hurry, so let's _____ our time and enjoy the trip.

4   When I heard what he said, it _____ me smile.

5   My grandfather _____ his driving test when he was 75!

6   Learning the guitar was difficult at first, but now I'm _____ a lot of progress.

7   If you have a better idea, please feel free to _____ a suggestion!

8   He's interested in other people and _____ friends easily.

9   My sister _____ an interest in her friends. They all like her. | 8 |

How did you do?

Total: | 25 |

| :) | Very good 25 – 20 | :| | OK 19 – 16 | :(| Review Unit 8 again 15 or less |

Vocabulary bank

Unit 3 phrases with *get*

1 to get home = to arrive at your home
    I usually **get home** from school at about five o'clock.

2 to get together = to meet with other people
    My friends and I **get together** on Sundays to play soccer in the park.

3 to get a [phone] call
    I **got** five **calls** last night while I was working.

4 to get sick
    When we were on vacation, my sister **got sick** because she drank water from the faucet.

5 to get somewhere/anywhere = to improve, to make progress
    I started learning Spanish last year, but I'm not **getting anywhere** so I think I'll stop.

6 to get hot/cold/warm
    It's **getting** really **cold** now. Let's go back into the house.

7 to get hungry/thirsty
    I'm **getting hungry**. Can we have lunch soon?

8 to get going = to start (something) / to leave
    Look! It's almost ten o'clock. I think we should **get going**, or we'll be late.

9 to get a/the chance
    I'm really busy now, but I'll call you if I **get a chance**.

10 to get pleasure (from)
    I'm not very good at table tennis, but I **get** a lot of **pleasure** from playing it.

Unit 4 sports

1 a stadium
    The **stadium** holds 60,000 people.

2 a championship
    He won the **championship** for the fifth time.

3 to score
    He **scored** a great goal.

4 a goal/point
    In soccer, you score **goals**, and in basketball you score **points**.

5 to tie / a tie
    The game was **tied**, 3–3. It was a tie.

6 a reserve
    I didn't play. I was a **reserve**.

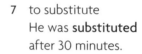

7 to substitute
    He was **substituted** after 30 minutes.

8 a record
    It's a new world **record**!

9 to hold a/the record
    He **holds the record** for the marathon.

10 to break a record
    She **broke** the world record for the 100-meter race.

Unit 6 North American and British English

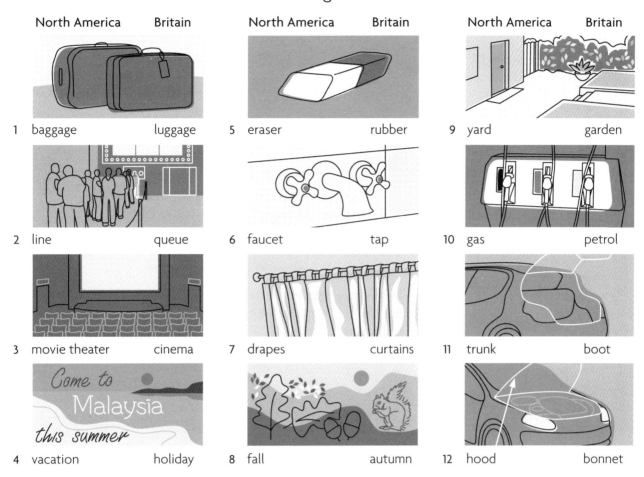

	North America	Britain		North America	Britain		North America	Britain
1	baggage	luggage	5	eraser	rubber	9	yard	garden
2	line	queue	6	faucet	tap	10	gas	petrol
3	movie theater	cinema	7	drapes	curtains	11	trunk	boot
4	vacation	holiday	8	fall	autumn	12	hood	bonnet

Unit 7 talking about age

1 adulthood = the time of life when you are an adult
   Adulthood brings responsibility.

2 childhood = the time of life when you are a child
   She didn't have a very happy **childhood**.

3 adolescence = the time of life when you are a teenager/adolescent
   Some people think **adolescence** is the best time of your life!

4 youth = the time of life when you are young
   My grandmother says the world was very different **in her youth**.

5 to get/grow old(er)
   My dad always says he isn't worried about **getting older**.

6 to be getting on = to get/grow old
   He was a good athlete when he was 25, but he's **getting on** in years now.

7 underage = too young to do something (because of a law)
   You have to be 16 to watch that movie. I'm only 15, so I'm **underage**.

8 to come of age = to reach the age when you are legally an adult
   In most states in the U.S., people **come of age** when they are 18.

9 to look [your] age = to look the age that you really are
   He looks like he's 20, but really he's 40! He doesn't **look his age** at all.

10 to act [your] age = <u>not</u> to behave as if you were a child (or younger than you really are)
   Oh, Jimmy! You're not six years old any more! You're 15! **Act your age**!

Unit 8 – verb and noun pairs

have

1 an accident
James is in the hospital. He **had an accident** in his car.

2 a problem
I **have a problem**. I want to buy that shirt, but I don't have any money.

3 an idea
We didn't know what to do, but then Alice **had an idea**.

4 a meal
Last night we all went out to a restaurant and **had a** really nice **meal** together.

make

5 a suggestion = to suggest
Can I **make a suggestion**? Why don't we go to the movies tonight?

6 an offer = to offer
I didn't want to sell my bike, but somebody **made** me **an offer** of $100, so I sold it.

7 a decision = to decide
I don't know which one to buy, but I need to **make a decision** quickly.

8 progress = to get better
My German is getting better and better. I'm **making** a lot of **progress**.

take

9 a test / an exam = to take a test
My mother **took** her driving **test** last week and she passed!

10 [your] time = not to do something quickly
We aren't late, so we can **take** our **time** and not hurry.

11 a break = to stop work for a short time
We worked for three hours, and then we **took a break** and had some coffee.

12 an interest [in] = show interest
We really like our teacher because she **takes an interest** in all of us.

Grammar reference

Unit 3

Past continuous

1 We use the past continuous to talk about actions in progress at a certain time in the past.
*In 1999, we **were living** in California.   The television was on, but I **wasn't watching** it.*

2 The past continuous is formed with the simple past of *be* + verb + *-ing*.
*You **were running** very fast.*   *You **weren't running** very fast.*
*Andy **was listening** to the radio.*   *Andy **wasn't watching** television.*

3 The question is formed with the simple past of *be* + subject + verb + *-ing*.
***Was** James **running**?*   *Yes, he **was**. / No, he **wasn't**.*
***Were** your parents **having** lunch?*   *Yes, they **were**. / No, they **weren't**.*
*What **were** you **studying**?*
*Why **was** she **crying**?*

Past continuous vs. simple past

1 When we talk about the past, we use the simple past for actions that happened at one particular time. We use the past continuous for background actions.
*When my friend **arrived**, I **was having** lunch.   He **was driving** too fast, and he **had** an accident.*
*What **did** you **say**? I **wasn't listening**.*

2 We often use *when* with the simple past and *while* with the past continuous.
*I was sleeping **when** the phone rang.   **While** Jack was washing the dishes, he dropped a plate.*

Unit 4

Comparative and superlative adjectives

1 When we want to compare two things, or two groups of things, we use a comparative form + *than*.
*I'm **taller than** my father.   DVDs are **more expensive than** CDs.   His watch is **better than** mine.*

2 With short adjectives, we normally add *-er*: *cold – colder   long – longer   smart – smarter*

If the adjective ends in *e*, we add only *-r*: *white – whiter   safe – safer*

If the adjective ends with consonant + *-y*, we change the *y* to *i* and add *-er*.
easy – easier   early – earlier   happy – happier

If the adjective ends in one vowel + one consonant, we double the final consonant and add *-er*.
big – bigger   fat – fatter   thin – thinner

3 With longer adjectives (two or more syllables), we use *more* + the adjective.
*expensive – **more** expensive   boring – **more** boring*

4 Some adjectives have a different comparative form.
*good – **better**   bad – **worse**   far – **farther***

5 We can modify the comparison by using *much*, *a lot* or *a little*. These words come before the normal comparison.
*This movie is **much** better than the book.   His pronunciation is **a lot** worse than mine.*
*We walked **a little** farther today than last week.*

Adverbs

1 We use adverbs to describe verbs. Adverbs say how an action is or was performed.
*She <u>smiled</u> **happily**.   <u>Drive</u> **slowly**!   We <u>got</u> to school **late**.*

We can also use adverbs before adjectives.
*It was **bitterly** <u>cold</u> yesterday.   The water was **incredibly** <u>warm</u>, so we went swimming.*

2   Most adverbs are formed by adjective + -ly: *quiet – quietly*   *bad – badly*

If the adjective ends in -le, we drop the -e and add -y: *terrible – terribly*   *comfortable – comfortably*

If the adjective ends in consonant + -y, we change the y to i and add -ly.
easy – easily   *happy – happily*   *lucky – luckily*

3   Some adverbs are irregular. They don't have an -ly ending.
*good – **well*****   ***fast – fast*****   ***hard – hard*****   ***early – early*****   *late – **late***

Comparative adverbs

1   To compare adverbs, we use the same rules as we do when we compare adjectives. With short adverbs that don't end in -ly, we add -er or -r, and *than* after the adverb.
*I was late for school, but my brother was **later than** me!*

2   With longer adverbs, we use *more* + adverb + *than*.
*I ran **more quickly than** the others.*

3   To compare the adverb *well*, we use *better … than*. To compare the adverb *far*, we use *farther … than*.
*Steve plays tennis **better than** I do.*   *My school is **farther** from my house **than** the park.*

Unit 5

will/won't, or *might (not) / may (not)* for prediction

1   We can use the modal verb *will ('ll)* or *will not (won't)* to make predictions about the future.
*Don't worry about the exam next week. It **won't be** difficult.*

2   We use *might/might not* or *may/may not* to make less certain predictions about the future.
*I'm not sure, but I think I **might go** to college when I finish high school.*

3   Like all modal verbs, *will/won't* and *might/might not* and *may/may not* are followed by the base form of the main verb, and the form is the same for all subjects.
*I think it'**ll be** a nice day tomorrow.* (**NOT** ~~I think it'll to be a nice day tomorrow.~~)
*My brother **might go** to live in Europe.* (**NOT** ~~My brother might to go to live in Europe.~~)
*She **may not pass** her driving test.*

4   We make questions with *will* by putting the subject **after** the modal verb.
***Will** we **have** a test next week?*

First conditional

1   We often make conditional sentences by using *If* + subject + present simple in the *if* clause and *will/won't / might/might not* in the main clause.
*If we **have** time, **we'll do** some shopping at the supermarket.*
*I **might go** out tonight **if there's** nothing good on TV.*

2   We can also use the word *unless* in conditional sentences. It means *if … not*.
***Unless** the teacher explains, we won't know what to do.* (= **If** the teacher **doesn't** explain, we won't know what to do.)
*James won't know **unless** you tell him.* (= James won't know **if** you **don't** tell him.)

3   There are two clauses in these sentences. We can put the main clause first, or the *if/unless* clause first. When the *if/unless* clause comes first, there is a comma after it.
Unless the teacher explains, we won't know what to do.
We won't know what to do unless the teacher explains.

Unit 6

Tag questions

1   Tag questions are affirmative or negative questions at the end of statements. We add "tags" to the end of statements:

a)   when **we are not sure** that what we are saying is correct, and we want the other person to say if we are correct or not.

b)   when **we are almost sure** that what we are saying is correct, and we want the other person to confirm it.

2   Tags in (a) above have rising intonation: *A: You're French, **aren't you**?*   *B: No, I'm not. I'm Swiss.*

Tags in (b) above have falling intonation: *A: You're French, **aren't you**?*   *B: Yes. I'm from Lyon.*

3   With **affirmative** statements, we use a **negative** tag question: *I'm late, **aren't I**?*   *He's lazy, **isn't he**?*

With **negative** statements, we use an **affirmative** tag question: *I'm not late, **am I**?*   *He isn't lazy, **is he**?*

Present perfect

1   We use the present perfect (present tense of *have* + past participle) to talk about a present situation, and the events in the past that are connected to the present situation.
    *The teacher's angry because we **haven't done** our homework.   I**'ve eaten** too much food, and I **feel** sick.*

2   There is an important difference between *have gone* and *have been*.
    *My friend Sarah **has been** to Peru on vacation. (= Sarah went to Peru, <u>and she has come back again</u>.)*
    *My friend Sarah **has gone** to Peru on vacation. (= Sarah went to Peru, and <u>she is still there</u>.)*

Present perfect + *already/yet/just*

1   We often use the words *already* and *yet* with the present perfect. We use *already* in affirmative sentences and *yet* in negative sentences and in questions.

    The word *already* usually comes between *have* and the past participle. The word *yet* usually comes at the end of the sentence or question.
    *I don't want to watch the movie on TV tonight. I**'ve already seen** it.*
    *I started this work two hours ago, but I **haven't finished** it **yet**.*

2   When we use the word *just* with the present perfect, it means "not very long ago." Like *already*, *just* is usually placed between *have* and the past participle.
    *I**'ve just heard** that my favorite band has released a new CD.*
    *Do you want a piece of cake? My mother**'s just made it**.*

Unit 7

Present passive

1   We use the passive when it isn't important to know who does the action, or when we don't know who does it.
    *A lot of movies **were made** about the war. (It's not important to know who made them.)*
    *That house **was built** in 1852. (I don't know who built it.)*

2   To form the present passive, we use the simple present of the verb *to be* + the past participle
    of the main verb: *Soccer **is played** in many countries.   The animals in the zoo **are fed** every day.*

let/be allowed to

1   We use *be allowed to* to say that you do (or don't) have permission to do something.
    *At my school, we **are allowed to** wear jeans.   You **aren't allowed to** skateboard in the park.*

2   We use *let* to say that someone gives you, or doesn't give you, permission to do something.
    *I **let** my brother borrow my bicycle sometimes.   Our teacher **didn't let** us use dictionaries for the test.*

3   Both *let* and *be allowed to* are followed by the infinitive.
    *I'm not allowed to **watch** the late-night movie.   My dad didn't let me **watch** the late-night movie.*

4   With *let*, the structure is *let* + person + the base form of the verb (without *to*).
    *She **didn't let me answer** the question.   I'm not going to **let you borrow** my CD player.*

Unit 8

Present perfect with *for* and *since*

1   We can use the present perfect to talk about something that began in the past and continues to be true in the present.
    *I **have lived** here for ten years. (= I started living here ten years ago, and I still live here.)*

2   We talk about the time between when something started and now with *for* or *since*.

    We use the word *for* when we mention **a period of time** from the past until now.
    *for **an hour**   for **two years**   for **a long time***

    We use the word *since* when we mention a **point in time** in the past.
    *since **ten o'clock**   since **1992**   since **last Saturday***

Notes

Notes

Notes

Thanks and acknowledgments

The authors would like to thank a number of people whose support has proved invaluable during the planning, writing and production process of *American English in Mind*.

First of all we would like to thank the numerous teachers and students in many countries of the world who have used the first edition of *English in Mind*. Their enthusiasm for the course, and the detailed feedback and valuable suggestions we got from many of them were an important source of inspiration and guidance for us in developing the concept and in the creation of *American English in Mind*.

In particular, the authors and publishers would like to thank the following teachers who gave up their valuable time for classroom observations, interviews and focus groups:

Brazil

Warren Cragg (ASAP Idiomas); Angela Pinheiro da Cruz (Colégio São Bento; Carpe Diem); Ana Paula Vedovato Maestrello (Colégio Beatíssima Virgem Maria); Natália Mantovanelli Fontana (Lord's Idiomas); Renata Condi de Souza (Colégio Rio Branco, Higienópolis Branch); Alexandra Arruda Cardoso de Almeida (Colégio Guilherme Dumont Villares / Colégio Emilie de Villeneuve); Gisele Siqueira (Speak Up); Ana Karina Giusti Mantovani (Idéia Escolas de Línguas); Maria Virgínia G. B. de Lebron (UFTM / private lessons); Marina Piccinato (Speak Up); Patrícia Nero (Cultura Inglesa / Vila Mariana); Graziela Barroso (Associação Alumni); Francisco Carlos Peinado (Wording); Maria Lúcia Sciamarelli (Colégio Divina Providencia / Jundiaí); Deborah Hallal Jorge (Nice Time Language Center); Lilian Itzicovitch Leventhal (Colégio I. L. Peretz); Dulcinéia Ferreira (One Way Línguas); and Priscila Prieto and Carolina Cruz Marques (Seven Idiomas).

Colombia

Luz Amparo Chacón (Gimnasio Los Monjes); Mayra Barrera; Diana de la Pava (Colegio de la Presentación Las Ferias); Edgar Ardila (Col. Mayor José Celestino Mutis); Sandra Cavanzo B. (Liceo Campo David); Claudia Susana Contreras and Luz Marina Zuluaga (Colegio Anglo Americano); Celina Roldán and Angel Torres (Liceo Cervantes del Norte); Nelson Navarro; Maritza Ruiz Martín; Francisco Mejía, and Adriana Villalba (Colegio Calasanz).

Ecuador

Paul Viteri (Colegio Andino, Quito); William E. Yugsan (Golden Gate Academy – Quito); Irene Costales (Unidad Educativa Cardinal Spellman Femenino); Vinicio Sanchez and Sandra Milena Rodríguez (Colegio Santo Domingo de Guzmán); Sandra Rigazio and María Elena Moncayo (Unidad Educativa Tomás Moro, Quito); Jenny Alexandra Jara Recalde and Estanislao Javier Pauta (COTAC, Quito); Verónica Landázuri and Marisela Madrid (Unidad Educativa "San Francisco de Sales"); Oswaldo Gonzalez and Monica Tamayo (Angel Polibio Chaves School, Quito); Rosario Llerena and Tania Abad (Isaac Newton, Quito); María Fernanda Mármol Mazzini and Luis Armijos (Unidad Educativa Letort, Quito); and Diego Bastidas and Gonzalo Estrella (Colegio Gonzaga, Quito).

Mexico

Connie Alvarez (Colegio Makarenko); Julieta Zelinski (Colegio Williams); Patricia Avila (Liceo Ibero Mexicano); Patricia Cervantes de Brofft (Colegio Frances del Pedregal); Alicia Sotelo (Colegio Simon Bolivar); Patricia Lopez (Instituto Mexico, A.C.); Maria Eugenia Fernandez Castro (Instituto Oriente Arboledas); Lilian Ariadne Lozano Bustos (Universidad Tecmilenio); Maria del Consuelo Contreras Estrada (Liceo Albert Einstein); Alfonso Rene Pelayo Garcia (Colegio Tomas Alva Edison); Ana Pilar Gonzalez (Instituto Felix de Jesus Rougier); and Blanca Kreutter (Instituto Simon Bolivar).

Our heartfelt thanks go to the *American English in Mind* team for their cooperative spirit, their many excellent suggestions and their dedication, which have been characteristic of the entire editorial process: Paul Phillips, Amy E. Hawley, Kelley Perrella, Eric Zuarino, Pam Harris, Kate Powers, Brigit Dermott, Kate Spencer, Heather McCarron, Keaton Babb, Roderick Gammon, Hugo Loyola, Howard Siegelman, Colleen Schumacher, Margaret Brooks, Kathryn O'Dell, Genevieve Kocienda, Lisa Hutchins, and Lynne Robertson.

We would also like to thank the teams of educational consultants, representatives and managers working for Cambridge University Press in various countries around the world. Space does not allow us to mention them all by name here, but we are extremely grateful for their support and their commitment.

In Student's Book 2, thanks go to David Crystal for the interview in Unit 9, and to Jon Turner for giving us the idea of using the story of Ulises de la Cruz in Unit 15.

Thanks to the team at Pentacor Big for giving the book its design; the staff at Full House Productions for the audio recordings; and Lightning Pictures and Mannic Media for the video.

Last but not least, we would like to thank our partners, Mares and Adriana, for their support.

The publishers are grateful to the following illustrators: Ifan Bates (NB Illustration), Vanessa Bell (NB Illustration), Mark Blade (New Division), Matt Buckingham (Arena), Rosa Dodd (NB Illustration), Mark Duffin, Kel Dyson (Bright), Katie Evans (Folio), Dylan Gibson, Clementine Hope (NB Illustration),
Helen James (New Division), Graham Kennedy, David McAllister (NB Illustration), Paul McCaffrey (Sylvie Poggio), Clare Nicholas (New Division), Red Jelly Illustration, Sean Simms (New Division), Sharon Tancredi (Folio), Lucy Truman (New Division), Phil Wrigglewart (NB Illustration), David Young (NB Illustration)

The publishers are grateful to the following for permission to reproduce copyright photographs and material:

Key: l = left, c = center, r = right, t = top, b = bottom, u = upper, lo = lower, f = far

Student's Book

Alamy/©blickwinkel p 34 (crt, cl), /©Tibor Bognar p 49 (r), /©Graham Corney p 31 (cr), /©Chris Fredriksson p 34 (l), /©Tim Graham pp 34 (c), 36 (b/©ICP p 30 (l), /©Images & Stories p 44 (tl), /©Alan Williams p 30 (tr); /©Everett Kennedy Brown/epa p 49 (bl), /©moodboard p 34 (bl), /©Jose Fuste Raga p 30 (br), Education Photos/John Walmsley pp 31 (tr), FLPA/Mike Parry/Minden Pictures p 44 (br); /Natalie Behring-Chisholm p 3 (photo 5), /AFP/Frederic J.Brown p 24, /Mark Dadswell p 22 (bl), / Panoramic Images p 36 (loc), / Photographer's Choice/John William Banagan p 34 (crb), /Andreas Rentz p 31 (bl), /Stone/joSon p 38, /Stone/Romilly Lockyer p 46 (cr), /Taxi/ Maren Caruso p 46 (br), /Taxi/Reggie Casagrande p 46 (bc), /Taxi/Chris Clinton p 47, /Taxi/Ron and Patty Thomas p 36 (uc), /UpperCut Images p 46 (c), / iStock p 48, (cr), /ryasick p 48 (tr), /UnoPix p 48 (br); Photolibrary.com p 21 (b) /Doc-Stock/INSADCO Photography p 31 (tl), /White/C Squared Studios p 20 (l), /Jonathan Hordle p 21 (c), Science & Society Picture Library/ Science Museum p 20 (r); /bociek666 p 46 (cl), /Amy Nichole Harris p 36 (tl), Junial Enterprises p 3 (photo 6), /Luminis 46 (bl), /Vyacheslav Osokin p 31 (cl), / Alexander Raths p 3 (photo 1), /S.M. p 3 (photo 3), Dmitriy Shironosov p 3 (photo 4), /SPbPhoto p 21 (t), /Edwin Verin p 36 (tr), / Artmann Witte p 3 (photo 2); Still Pictures/©Ron Giling p 34 (br).

Getty Images/©Blend Images/Ross Anderson p 2 (laptop), AP Photo/©Skip Peterson p 6 (l), Getty Images/Photographer's Choice/©Peter Dazeley p 6 (tr), Alamy/©Red Cover p 6 (cr), Alamy/©Buzzshotz p 10 (t), Alamy/©Peter Casolino p 14 (tr), Alamy/©Chuck Eckert p 14 (cr), Shutterstock/©tadija p 16 (wipers), / Shutterstock/©Baloncici p 16 (engine), Shutterstock/©Oliver Hoffmann p 16 (mousetrap), / Shutterstock/©Johnny Habell p 16 (dishwasher), Shutterstock/©bhowe p 16 (kitchen), Shutterstock p 16 (remote), Shutterstock/©Coprid p 16 (gum), Shutterstock/©ZTS p 16 (skates), Getty Images/AFP/©Mark Ralston p 22 (Prado),Getty Images/©Stu Forster p 22 (Obergföl), AP Photo/©Ng Han Guan p 22 (Velazco), Alamy/©Jim Lane p 28 (tr&c), Alamy/©Alex Segre p 31 (bl), Shutterstock/©iofoto p 48 (bl), Getty Images/©Stephen Brashear p 50 (b), Getty Image/Workbook Stock/©Lori Adamski Peek p 51 (l), istockphoto.com/©Aldo Murillo p 56 (l), istockphoto.com

Workbook

Alamy/Lynden Pioneer Museum p 17 (tr); Corbis/©David Ball/amanaimages p 29 (t), /©Jerry Cooke p 41 (br), /©Turba p 41; FLPA/Minden Pictures/ Mike Parryp 38; Getty Images/AFP/EVARISTO SA p 41 (l), /AFP/ Timothy Clary p 41 (tc), /Photographer's Choice/Jeff Hunter p 28, iStockphoto/Yuri Arcurs p 42, Masterfile p 44; /Stockbroker/Monkey Business Images Ltd p 22; Planetary Visions Ltd/Science Photo Library p 29 (b); Press Association Images/AP/Dolores Ochoa R. p 48, /Shutterstock Images/Nejat p 17 (l), / Serbin Dmitry p 17 (br).

Getty Images/Carlsson, Peter/Johner Images p5; Getty Images/Comstock Images p6;

Loc8tor Ltd. p12 (t); TrackItBack.com Inc. p12 (b);

The publishers are grateful to the following for their assistance with commissioned photographs:

Mannic Media

Song / text acknowledgments

Big Yellow Taxi on p.31 Words and music by Joni Mitchell. Copyright © 1970 (renewed) Crazy Crow Music. All Rights Administered by Sony/ATV Music Publishing, 8 Music Square West, Nashville, TN 37203. All Rights Reserved. Used by permission of Alfred Publishing Co Inc. Recording copyright © Marathon Media International.

Don't Worry Be Happy on p 49. Words & Music by Bobby McFerrin Copyright © 1988 Prob Noblem Music, USA. Universal Music Publishing MGB Limited. Used by permission of Music Sales Limited. All Rights Reserved. International Copyright Secured. All rights administered in the US and Canada by Universal – Careers Music (BMI). Recording copyright © Marathon Media International.

Chuy Varela for the adapted text on p 75 'Music that changes lives' from an article 'An Afro-Brazilian Keeper of the Flame' from *San Francisco Chronicle*, 10 June 2007. Reproduced by permission of Chuy Varela.

DVD-ROM Instructions

American English in Mind can be run directly from the DVD-ROM and does not require installation. However, you can also install *American English in Mind* and run it from your hard drive. This will make the DVD-ROM run more quickly.

Start the DVD-ROM

Windows PC

- Insert the *American English in Mind* DVD-ROM into your DVD-ROM drive.
- If Autorun is enabled, the DVD-ROM will start automatically.
- If Autorun is not enabled, open **My Computer** and then **D:** (where D is the letter of your DVD-ROM drive). Then double click on the *American English in Mind* icon.

Mac OS X

- Insert the *American English in Mind* DVD-ROM into your DVD-ROM drive.
- Double-click on the DVD-ROM icon on your desktop to open it.
- Double-click on the *American English in Mind* Mac OS X icon.

Install the DVD-ROM to your hard drive (recommended)

Windows PC

- Go to **My Computer** and then **D:** (where D is the letter of your DVD-ROM drive).
- Right-click on *Explore*.
- Double-click on *Install American English in Mind to hard drive*.
- Follow the installation instructions on your screen.

Mac OS X

- Double-click on the DVD-ROM icon on your desktop to open it.
- Create a folder on your computer.
- Copy the content of the DVD-ROM into this folder.
- Double-click on the *American English in Mind* Mac OS X icon.

Listen and practice on your CD player

You can listen to and practice language from the Student's Book Pronunciation, Culture in Mind and Photostory activities. You can also listen to and practice the Workbook Pronunciation and Listening activities.

What's on the DVD-ROM?

- **Interactive practice activities**
  Extra practice of Grammar, Vocabulary, English Pronunciation, Reading and Writing. Click on a set of unit numbers (1–2 through 15–16) at the top of the screen. Then choose an activity and click on it to start.

- **Word list**
  Pronunciation and definitions. Click on *Word list* on the left side of the screen. Then choose a word to hear its pronunciation. You can also add your own notes.

- **Self-test**
  Click on *Self-test*, and choose a set of unit numbers (1–2 through 15–16) on the left side of the screen. You can also test yourself on multiple sets of units.

- **Game**
  This is extra practice of Grammar and Vocabulary. Click on the game controller icon at the top of the screen. Click on a set of unit numbers (1–2 through 15–16), and choose a character. Click on start to begin the game. You can also choose all the units.

System Requirements

- 512MB of RAM (1GB recommended for video)
- 1GB free hard disk space (if installing to hard disk)
- 800 x 600 resolution or higher
- speakers or headphones
- a microphone if you wish to record yourself speaking

For PC

- Windows XP, Vista or 7

For Mac

- Mac OSX 10.4 or 10.5
- 1.2 GHz G4 processor or higher

Support

If you experience difficulties with this DVD-ROM, please visit: http://www.cambridge.org/elt/multimedia/help